Walking in
HOPE, Living in
GRACE
THE TAPESTRY

MARYALYCE POOLE

BALBOA
PRESS
A DIVISION OF HAY HOUSE

Balboa Press books may be ordered through booksellers or by contacting:

Balboa Press
A Division of Hay House
1663 Liberty Drive
Bloomington, IN 47403
www.balboapress.com
1 (877) 407-4847

Cover design by Michael Hartsock

Printed in the United States of America.

ISBN: 978-1-4525-9539-9 (sc)
ISBN:978-1-4525-9541-2 (hc)
ISBN: 978-1-4525-9540-5 (e)

Library of Congress Control Number: 2014906129

Balboa Press rev. date: 4/15/2014

CONTENTS

DEDICATED TO THOSE who have held on to *hope* for me for so many years:

TO MY PARENTS, family, the children I love, (Pam, Troy, and Steven), friends, the Cursillo community, my coworkers, mental health professionals, and spiritual director (Father Peter Creed); to Mike Walsh, for editing this venture of hope; and to Jesus Christ, the center of my hope.

INTRODUCTION

JUGGLING TIME AND place had become difficult for me. My world seemed to be out of control. The only way to regain control would be to put on my bathing suit and swim, as I had when I was a teenage junior lifeguard in Henrico County, Virginia. I backed into a dirt road to hide from the world. It was a warm day, and I stopped to get my thoughts together. But the time slipped away; before I knew it I was late for work, something that rarely happened.

I burst into the president's office and blurted out that I would be the next president of the company, the second-largest printing company on the East Coast. Using explicit language, I said a woman had never been president, and I would be the first. I became agitated and annoyed as he stayed calm. This episode didn't last very long; he told his secretary to phone my husband to come and get me.

I left in my little Datsun blue pickup truck and paid no mind to his statements of concern about my driving. The company had two facilities, and I drove to the second one, which was a little further east in downtown Richmond, Virginia. I burst in and announced that the building should be a school for printing. I gave the director of the facility a school bell, which I'd put into my briefcase that morning. Without giving him a chance to talk, I rambled on, describing how the school should look and explaining why a school for printing was so important. He offered to drive me home, but I escaped and drove myself back to the main facility.

By this time, everything appeared to be occurring in slow motion;

the faster I thought I was going, the slower I went. I returned to the parking lot of the main facility, unsure of what to do next: go back into the building or go to my husband's workplace just a few miles away.

My mind raced between thoughts of the punishment and not being able to focus on anything. The day was warming up, and I couldn't figure out how to operate the air conditioner. I drove to the automobile shop where my husband worked, very slowly and mostly on the wrong side of the road. I tried to remember a shortcut through the park and got lost just two miles from my destination.

When I arrived at the shop, my husband was busy with customers. So I went into the parts room and fell asleep standing up. I had not slept for three or four days. A little while later my next-door neighbor appeared and said he would take me home.

Riding home, I could hear his voice in my head; it kept getting louder. It told me I was a bad mother and wife, and that it was a good thing I could not have any more children. Yet I can't recall saying anything.

I went into the house and took three darts from the dartboard and threw them at his back door. I went back into my house and cried. I was very confused and saw flashes of colored lights go past my window. Filled with remorse, I went to my neighbor's backdoor and replaced the darts with bells.

My neighbor's wife was a nurse, and she had returned home from work. My husband was home also. It was late in the afternoon, and their focus was on getting me to a hospital. From my bedroom window, I saw the three of them having a conversation, I knew it was about me, but I was busy removing my clothes, then putting them back on, over and over again.

Through the window, I could see them pointing at me. I went out of my bedroom and through the front door into the patch of woods beyond the front yard. My head was racing and felt big, bigger than life itself. I went out to the street and sat in the ditch. I got up and took off my shorts and top and, now naked, put my arms and hands up to stop the traffic. That seemed to bring me relief.

I went back into the woods and put my clothes on. I heard someone calling my name and walked slowly around to the back of the house. My husband asked me where I wanted to go. I said, "Church." My husband and my neighbors took me to Westbrook Hospital in Richmond.

I had been betrayed! They persuaded me to go into the lobby. I would not stay. I kicked, bit, yelled, and screamed. My first husband had left me while I was in the hospital for situational depression. The nurse tried to give me an injection, and I knocked it out of her hand. I was not about to stay voluntarily.

My neighbor went to the magistrate's office in Henrico County, Virginia, to obtain a green warrant to admit me non-voluntarily to the hospital. A Henrico police officer escorted my husband and me to Saint Mary's Hospital. I was held down in the back of the police vehicle. I relaxed in my husband's arms and was taken to the psychiatric intensive care unit (ICU). I lost all sense of time and remember waking up in a small padded room with a small window on the door. The light switch was outside the room and was controlled by the staff. I would bang on the door to get them to keep the light on, so I could distinguish between day and night. My confusion about the time was compounded by medication and sleep. It was hard to think.

Three days later, I found myself sitting at a table in the psychiatric unit with the police officer who brought me into the hospital, a special judge who didn't look like a judge, and a lawyer who was there to represent me (although I had never seen or talked to him before that day). There were other people in the room, but I don't remember who they were or why they were there.

They read the allegations against me. I felt like a criminal who had not committed any crime. I did not drink, yet I felt as though I had a hangover—addled and in a cloud, consumed by unconnected thoughts. I had to admit I had a mental illness, manic depression, which I'd never heard of before. I didn't even know what the spokesperson for the group was talking about. They talked about moving me somewhere else; I feared it was to another padded cell. I was frightened and confused about what would happen to me next.

Who Was I?

Who was I, and what was I doing when the clouds began to form? Who was I, and what was I doing when the clouds began to turn dark? Who was I, and what was I doing when the lightning flashed and the thunder began to sound? I was confused. From which direction did the lightning and thunder come? My head hurt so badly; the pain was almost unbearable. My mind kept repeating over and over: how loud and how long will this thunder storm last? How long will the pain last? The clouds were full, the rain poured down, and the tears poured out for help, and I said, *Who am I, and what am I doing?* The clouds started to break up, and the rain ended. The clouds were just as empty as my heart and my head. In the emptiness, I could hear God calling my name. It is only after the storm, after the lighting, thunder, and rain, that we fill back up from the emptiness. It is in the broken clouds that we have rain and in the broken grain that we have bread. It takes a broken person to reach out for help, to reach up to the One who returns a greater power than an individual ever had. I now have hope and am helping and educating myself, family, and friends; we are overcoming the barriers and preventing the pain. I come to you in remission from manic depression (bipolar disorder). I ask you to wear a yellow ribbon for hope, so that those who are broken will become whole and their personal storms will fill up with the light from the sun and the Son.

The Tapestry

I use HOPE as an acronym for:

Helping yourself first, to obtain the hope that you dream for yourself, then share it with others

Overcoming the barriers, as we all have them

Preventing mental pain through prayer, prescriptions, and psychiatrists

Educating yourself; learn about yourself first, then share with others

Go through this journey of HOPE with me. It is not a destination, because each new hope brings us to a new destination.

CHAPTER 1
HOPE IN FAMILY

Who am I on this journey of hope?

THE HILLS WERE alive but not with the sound of music. A father was driving his colicky baby girl around the Pocono Mountains. Riding in the car soothed the child and lessened the wailing. Only a few weeks old, the baby girl's name was Lynedithclar. Her mother was upset and suffered from a mental-health problem called melancholia. The birth certificate had already been issued, and the baby girl was to be baptized in a few weeks. The mother would not respond to her husband's questions about why she was so melancholy. A few days before the baptism, the mother aggressively stated that she did not like the baby's chosen name and wanted to name her after herself and her best friend. Thus, the name on my birth certificate was changed to Maryalyce Budjinski. The first of my many name changes occurred before I was even one month old. I was baptized and confirmed as Maryalyce on May 16, 1948, by Reverend Michael Oleksew at Saints Peter and Paul Ukrainian Greek Catholic Church in Wilkes-Barre, Pennsylvania. It was a bit of a surprise that my godparents were Roman Catholic. My godmother was my father's sister; she and her fiancé would marry several months later. The Ukrainian Greek Catholic Church allows Roman Catholics to serve as godparents.

As a child, I found it hard to keep still. Perpetual motion was part of my life as a two-year-old. One time I jumped out of a highchair to greet my daddy and broke my collar bone. Keeping still was a real chore.

A different kind of moving—relocation—became part of the tapestry of my life. We moved from Trucksville, Pennsylvania, to Wyoming, Pennsylvania, when I was four years old.

Moving was part of my family history. My great-grandmother, Anna Opryazka, who I called Baba, came from Poland, and Githo, my great-grandfather, Anthony Opryazka, came from the Ukraine. Grandma Tedesco, Frances Ann Opryazka, was born in Peckville, Pennsylvania, and Grandpa Tedesco, Charles, was born in Genoa, Italy. Grandma Schrader Budjinski was born in Glen Lyon, Pennsylvania, and Grandpa Walter Budjinski (Budjizinski) was born in Poland. The spelling of his name was changed when he entered the United States at Ellis Island.

My maternal grandparents, Frances and Charles Tedesco, lived at Baba's house at 826 Ridge Road up on the mountain in Peckville, Pennsylvania. Grandpa Tedesco and I would walk through the woods, past the railroad tracks and over the creek toward Backeties, a beer garden, and Fred's, the candy store. Before Grandpa went into Backeties, he'd give me twenty-five cents to go to Fred's. Later, we'd meet outside the beer garden and walk back up the mountain. I wasn't afraid to walk to the candy store by myself. Grandpa said I had a good sense of direction and would be able to do anything I wanted.

I knew each rock along the path, the smell and placement of each tree and flower. Grandpa gave me the confidence to go down the mountain by myself. He knew about my imaginary friend, Judy, and told me it was okay. His friends were the parakeets that had saved his life more than once in the mines. Grandpa was a coal miner who raised the parakeets that descended into the mine with the men. If methane gas was present, the birds would get dizzy or die from the gas, alerting the men to the danger. Those birds he raised were a lifesaver. Sometimes Grandpa would say to me, "Judy will save your life from the cruel world."

When I was a little girl, our family celebrated two Christmases. My father's side of the family celebrated December 25, as they followed the traditions of the Roman Catholic Church. We exchanged gifts at our home in Wyoming; then we traveled to Peckville to visit with the rest of the Budjinski family.

Grandma and Grandpa Budjinski lived on Prospect Hill with my godparents, Aunt Clara and Uncle Marty. My father had eight brothers and sisters. Many of them lived out of state, and the snowy winters prevented the whole family from traveling to Peckville. On some holidays, it was just my brother and my parents.

The Christmas meal was brought from the kitchen on a cart and served on real china dishes. After dinner, the dishes were put back on the cart, wheeled to the kitchen, and put into one of the few electric dishwashers in town. There were two indoor bathrooms; to me, this made the house a mansion. Behind the house was a garage, and my grandparents raised pheasants in a pheasant coop. The Christmas tree was the largest tree that I'd ever seen indoors. A lot of the decorations were ornaments made by Aunt Clara's first-grade students.

Aunt Clara and Uncle Marty had American Kennel Club (AKC) registered Shelties. Grandpa Budjinski trained the dogs, since he was retired from the coal mines and was at home all day. The dogs were always well-behaved and had red bows around their necks at Christmas. They performed tricks my grandfather taught them.

I was amazed that the dogs never went into the living or dining area. Instead, they'd go up the backstairs in the kitchen, run down the hallway, and down the front stairs to the living room. Then, they would sit at the door, waiting to go out, as they had been taught. The dogs knew how to sit, stay, roll over, and come when called. I was thrilled that they even did tricks for me.

Still, when I was with the Budjinski side of family, I felt alone and believed that no one loved me. Grandma Budjinski would take me outside and pray with me: "Little Jesus, I am small; but to love you, I am tall." She noticed my isolation and came to my rescue in prayers.

We celebrated our other Christmas on January 6, with my mother's side of the family, the Tedescos. This was when the Ukrainian Church celebrated Little Christmas. Although it was not very big, the kitchen was where everyone gathered. Githo would take extra benches and chairs into the kitchen. Then hay was put down on the table and a white tablecloth put over the hay. The women prepared seven meatless entrees on a coal or wood stove. Before we ate, we prayed by passing around a square wafer (*oplatki*). Each person broke off a piece of *oplatki*, and after everyone had a piece, Grandmother Tedesco said the prayer. Along with the meal, there was a lot of wine, beer, and orange soda. My uncles, aunts, and cousins were always there.

We'd stay the night, and I slept on a warm *pinianta* (a homemade feather-tick bed) in a room over the kitchen. The downside of staying at Baba and Githo's house was the outdoor bathroom. I was afraid to use their two-hole outhouse because my brother teased that I would fall in. Sometimes I would wait several days until we got back to my house in Trucksville to go to the bathroom.

I grew up in two different worlds on opposite sides of the mountain, connected by a coal train. We visited that mountain often.

Hope, there is hope, dear God.

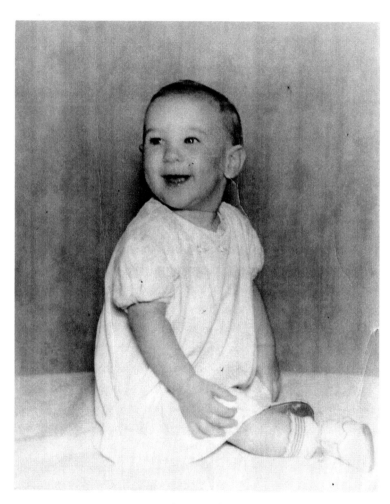

At the age of one.

Chapter 2
HOPE IN COMPANIONS

Who will journey with me?

MY DAD AND many of our friends and family built our house at 28 Clark Street in Wyoming, Pennsylvania. The house was near the Susquehanna River, high on a plateau; between the house and the river loomed a cliff and a flat plot of land.

As a child, I learned few social skills and did not have many friends. When I was five years old, Judy became my best friend. She had a place at the table and went on trips to my grandmother's house with me. When we where home we slept in a bedroom with a big bay window overlooking the Susquehanna River. I talked to Judy as if she were a real person. She even went to church with me. We went to Saint Joseph's Roman Catholic Church.

I slept with a light on because I was afraid someone might come into my bedroom. I was afraid of lightning and thunder, and I often headed for the closet during storms. My ten-year-old brother told me scary stories about Indians scalping little girls. As I screamed in fear, he'd turn the radio to *The Shadow* and *Dragnet*. Who ever got there first controlled what we heard that night. We rarely got to hear George Burns and Gracie Allen, my favorites.

When I was in kindergarten, we had to walk to school. But I would run because I was afraid the Indians would catch me. I sucked my thumb and curled my finger in my hair until my finger got caught and had to be cut loose. These habits persisted for a long time.

One day, Daddy brought home a box he called a television. It took two men to bring it in. As they unloaded it, they had to be careful not to break the tubes. He was excited, and I was too, until I saw nothing but a test pattern on the screen. We had to wait a couple of days until an antenna was attached and placed in the right location. When the black-and-white picture finally appeared, I still was not impressed. There were only a few stations, so I got bored quickly. I had more fun with Judy.

On Saturday mornings I went to Saint Joseph's for First Communion classes. I was given a book called *The Baltimore Catechism*, which was filled with questions and answers. The nun who taught us yelled out the questions, and we'd yell out the answers. When I got home, my mother yelled out the questions, and I'd yell out the answers again. It seemed to be a yelling match, and I had a lot of memorizing to do, which was very difficult for me. Judy knew, though; I asked her the questions, and she'd answer them. I didn't comprehend the information, but I knew the words that comprised the answers.

We talked about sin and going to confession. Everything I did seemed to be a sin. Each day, I practiced going to confession and communion. I memorized the act of contrition, so that I could say it by heart at my first confession and receive my First Communion.

My parents and family were so proud when I made my first communion; my mother brought me a girly white dress, white gloves, and white veil. Grandmother Budjinski gave me rosary beads that were the size of small marbles and even had my initials engraved on the crucifix. Saint Joseph's gave me a prayer book. My mother took me to a professional photographer several towns over. It was the first time we had pictures taken in a photography studio; in the past, photographers came to the house. Everyone was proud of me. I was proud of Judy for helping me to receive my First Communion.

While I walked to Wyoming Valley Elementary School, I talked to myself and Judy, and prayed that I would get there on time. I was known to procrastinate on the way to school. Once a week I would give the teacher ten cents to collect war-bond stamps. I was not sure what the purpose was, but it was fun to bring the book back to my parents with new stamps in it.

Dressed for my First Communion.

I went to a four-room schoolhouse for kindergarten, first grade, and part of second grade. When I was in second grade, my dad bought a small airport in Honesdale, Pennsylvania, and we moved into Baba's house in Peckville. Daddy and his friends remodeled the house; they converted the outdoor plumbing into indoor plumbing, put central heat in the house, and tore down the shanties that housed the chickens. They left the old barn intact, and the loft became my place. It was where Judy and I played school and had tea parties. The ladder was steep, but when I climbed up to the loft and looked out the door, I could see the whole world—the mountains and the train tracks. I would wave to the conductors as they passed by at eye level. The caboose conductor threw candy to my brother and me, as we waited for the train each day.

The milkman left several quarts of milk a day, and my brother, Robert, and I would race to bring them in. One day one of the bottles slipped out of Robert's hand, and he had to have stitches in his foot. We were not allowed to get the milk after that. The milkman brought a metal container and retrieved the empty bottles from the box every couple of days.

I went to Lincoln School for the second grade. The path to school down the mountain was the familiar one through the woods that I had taken so many times with my grandfather on the way to Backeties and Fred's. It was too far to walk home for lunch. I spent lunchtime with Grandma Tedesco. I would talk to the parakeets and listen to them cheep to each other. They kept me company at lunchtime. Grandma showed me how my grandpa put the birds to bed by covering the cage at night.

Christmas with Robert, 1954.

It wasn't that I disliked school; I just wasn't interested, although I tried hard. My teacher's name was Miss Tedesco (no relation, but she knew my Aunt Clara who taught second grade at Number One School). I wanted to do better, but I just didn't get it. I liked my imaginary world better.

Toward the end of the year, Miss Tedesco suggested that my parents take me to a child psychiatrist in Scranton. My parents followed her instructions and took me to a very large building with an elevator. This was frightening as I had never been in an elevator before; I was sure it would take me straight to heaven. The psychiatrist was sure I would outgrow my pretend friend and eventually catch up academically with class.

I looked forward to religious holidays. Sometimes we went to the Ukrainian church, Saints Cyril and Methodius Catholic Church in Olyphant, where my mother was raised; sometimes we went to Sacred Heart Roman Catholic Church in Peckville, where my father was raised. I think for convenience we went to Sacred Heart.

I sat prim and proper with Grandma Budjinski. If I didn't have a hat, Grandma pinned a hanky on my head. She liked when I went to church with her, and I liked being special to her. I can't remember going as a family, but Grandma Budjinski made sure I went with her. If I walked, I would meet her at church, or sometimes my aunt and uncle came by the house and blew the horn. I'd jump into the car real quick, as it was a skinny, two-way street on a hill, and only one car could go at a time.

During the season of Lent, schools let out early, and the Catholic children walked to church for the Stations of the Cross. This ritual was wonderful. I felt free to go to church by myself, and the church seemed to be happy for me to be there. It was a privilege. The church was big, with a red carpet, baptismal font, a large crucifix, and beautiful stained glass. I was sad to see Christ on the cross. Marking Christ's journey of Christ during the stations was also sad, but something drew me to this rite of the church, making me desire to go on my own.

My mother's Saints Cyril and Methodius Church was very different during holy days. The mass was in Ukrainian and was long. I didn't understand the language, but the ritual was an eye opener. It truly was beautiful—the church, the gold icons, and Communion, a piece of bread dipped in the wine, received on a spoon. At Easter, there was a blessing of the baskets with hard rolls; nut rolls; apricot rolls; braided bread with cheese and butter in the shape of lambs; kielbasa made by the town butcher; and beautiful *pysanka*, Easter eggs that told the story of the Ukrainian people. Daddy had to learn to dye the eggs to marry my mother, at least that's what I was told.

After the baskets were blessed, the people went into the church and walked on their knees from the back to the front of the church as a symbol of sacrifice. These people, mostly coal miners, sacrificed so much for their church.

We spent our summers on the Delaware River, with my parents' friends, my family, and my grandparents. Grandpa Tedesco taught me how to row a boat, by showing me first and then letting me try on my own. He watched me navigate that little boat up and down in front of the cottage for hours. He trusted that I could row that little boat where I wanted it to go. Grandpa would say, "Maryalyce, you don't have much book sense, but you will go further with common sense."

This place was like a cartoon cottage. My entire family, all of my parents' friends' families, and my grandparents all slept in the same room, and used one outhouse. If you had to go, you sat on a large rock out front until the person before you was finished; most of the time, I was pretty quick, because the smell was terrible.

We had breakfast and supper together, mostly the fish that had been caught that day. I learned to play cards (solitaire), and all the adults played pinochle in the evening under a dim light. There was no radio, no outside communication. And we called it fun.

Daddy got an interview with Trans World Airlines; he was excited because he thought he'd never get a job with a large company, even though Mom kept telling him he could do it. Lo and behold he got the job! This left Mom alone in the house with my brothers and me while Daddy went off to training school in Kansas City. Dad parked our turquoise Dodge in front of the house, just in case my mommy wanted to drive.

Change is a scary but necessary part of life. The outside world was trying to force change upon me, the more I spent time with Judy.

Hope is a journey of unfamiliarity, dear God.

CHAPTER 3
HOPE IN NEW PLACES

Where will this journey take me?

THAT SUMMER WENT by pretty quickly, but it was time to go to a school a little larger than that four-room schoolhouse. It probably had eight rooms. I could not have known I would be there for only two months.

It wasn't long before we found out that we were moving to another state; to me, it might well have been a different country. Daddy was transferred to Bloomfield, New Jersey, where he would be a flight engineer for TWA, Travel With Angles, my mother called it. So I packed up my dolls and told Judy we were taking a long trip.

My mother gave me a permanent that made my hair smell. I was not very happy. My aunt was a beautician and often practiced on me. Mommy also bought me new clothes at Scranton Dry Goods. Riding the bus to Scranton to shop had always been a treat, but while Dad was away, Mommy learned how to drive the car. The police officer across the street taught her, but she did not back up very well. We'd have to park blocks away from a store, so she could drive into a parking space and not have to back out. I liked that Mommy bought new things for me.

We made some quick overnight trips to Peckville. My brothers and

I stayed with our grandparents, so Mommy and Daddy could look for a house in Bloomfield. Mommy and Daddy said good-bye to their friends in Pennsylvania, and off we went to our new home.

It wasn't long before Daddy was gone for several days a time. He flew out of the Newark, LaGuardia, and Idlewild (now Kennedy) Airports. We had only one car, so if Mommy wanted to use it, she would have to drive him to and from the airport. Usually one of the kids would go with her, for security, she said, in case something happened to the car.

I couldn't see any mountains or rivers from my bedroom window; the topography in New Jersey was much different than in Pennsylvania. All I could see was a house with a backyard, tall hemlock trees with a badminton court behind them, and behind that a bridle path and a golf course, none of which I had seen before. The house smelled funny as the interior was made of chestnut wood, and there had been a chestnut tree blight the year the house was built. The basement was decorated and finished; we had rooms that were divided; and there was a laundry chute from the upstairs bathroom to the laundry room in the basement. The house even had sunroom in the back, surrounded by glass doors that slid open and shut. These were all foreign concepts to me. Maybe new was good?

Mommy registered Robert and me at Oakview Elementary School, which was about two blocks away. This school had twenty or more rooms. The principal had her own office. Robert was in kindergarten, and I was in the fourth grade. The teacher was very nice; after the first month, she had me tested for reading and math. The class was learning multiplications, and I did not know what a multiplication table was. I was reading at a second-grade level. This accelerated school had remedial classes for all subjects, and I was in all of them.

As I walked to the remedial classes, I was not alone, but I felt alone. The teacher was nice and took a lot of time with me, but I still felt unaccepted in the social realm. I was always the last one to be picked for kickball and was not asked to participate in afterschool activities. My mother enrolled me in Girl Scouts, but I felt as though I was on one side of a glass watching the others from a distance. I enjoyed the crafts, camping, and being part of a group, but earning Girl Scout badges was difficult for me. I could not shake the feeling that I was an outsider who was not accepted by my peers. I *was* accepted by the troop leaders. One leader sat on her front stoop and watched as I practiced roller skating to earn the skating badge. She exclaimed, "Hallelujah! You did it." I rolled back home feeling like I was skating on air.

My family starting going to Saint Thomas the Apostle Church on the Parkway. What a strange place. It had two masses going on at the same time. The children's Mass was in the basement of the church. Most of the girls sat together; a nun sat with us so we did not talk. I went to religious education at Saint Thomas on Wednesday afternoon after school and then walked home.

The first year was full of changes—new people; class trips on a chartered bus to Trenton to tour the historical sites; a teacher who taught a small group of students to read and write; and Mommy driving on the highway. Mommy also worked as a school traffic guard.

The second year I had a male teacher, which would never have happened in Peckville. I wasn't very good at classroom work, but I tried. My father would make games out of the schoolwork, like naming states and capitals; if I got them right, he'd let me ride with him to Willow Run Airport, Michigan, where my aunt and uncle lived, and he'd leave me there for the weekend.

One Easter the whole family went to Detroit for the holiday. While we were on the plane, I kept scratching my head and could not stop. After we were settled in my aunt's house, my dad noticed that I had bugs crawling on my head. I had lice! He shaved my head and then washed it with gasoline. My mother figured I got them when she took me shopping in New York City, and I tried on a lot of hats. Back then, little girls wore hats when they went to church. Going back to school without hair was terrible. I wore a hat until May. The boys tried to take my hat, but I was so embarrassed, that hat was on me to stay.

My brother and I went to public school, and our classes were filled with a diverse group of children. Students whose mothers worked could eat their packed lunches in the basement and purchase milk for five cents. Although my mother worked as a school traffic guard, I'd pick up my brother from his first-grade class and we'd walk home, where I'd put out the lunch Mommy left in the refrigerator. The only time we ate in the basement was when the weather was bad.

Unlike Peckville, the town was not completely Catholic. Some of my classmates talked about not having Christmas; they were Jewish and lit candles on a menorah. I couldn't understand how I had two Christmases, and they had none. I invited my Jewish friend to my Christmas, but she couldn't come. That made me sad.

I had been baptized in the Byzantine rite of the Catholic Church, where all the sacraments of initiation are received at birth, so the nuns asked me not to return to religious education class until the next year. The nuns, who never did anything wrong, asked me not to come back until after confirmation class. They explained that I was confirmed when I was baptized, but I didn't understand. I thought I'd been excommunicated from religious education and was teased by the other students in the class. What had I done that was so wrong? I loved going to church and often walked to Mass alone. Whenever I played school after this, I was not the nice nun I'd been before.

I had a new friend, Jill; her father was a minister and had his own study right in his house. Billy Graham was going to be at Madison Square Garden in New York City. Jill asked if I could go with her family. Well, it was a challenge to present this to my parents. I asked Mommy, who said ask Daddy. Daddy said ask Mommy, and so it went for several days. Daddy finally said yes, although he would be out of town.

So off we went to Madison Square Garden—Jill's parents, her five siblings, Jill, and me. We sat high up and listened to a lot of preaching, singing, amens, and hallelujahs. At the end Billy Graham asked for an altar call, and people swarmed down the steps. Jill's parents waited a long time, and then we all held hands and walked down the bleachers. Jill's parents and I were just singing away. I got up to Billy Graham and yelled at the top of my lungs, "Where's the altar rail?" Jill's father told Billy Graham that I was Catholic, and they moved me through very quickly.

School was tough. My fifth-grade teacher knew I was having difficulty with regular classes. He often had me stay after school to clean the blackboards and wash down the desks. I must have done that task pretty well; he wrote on my report card, "Maryalyce would make a good utility person."

That year I was asked to leave the Glee Club, because I could not sing. Afterschool baton lessons helped ease the disappointment and gave me something to do after school. Unfortunately, I was not coordinated enough to keep the baton from hitting me in the head. When I threw it up in the air, it hit my head more often than it did my hand.

Each Saturday, Mommy rotated with three other mothers, and they would take three young girls to the Upper Montclair YWCA. That is where I learned to swim. I enjoyed the water, and I went from pollywog (not knowing how to swim) to fish (swimming laps) in a year. After swimming lesson, we went to arts and crafts. The counselor showed us projects, and we talked about family and spirituality. We made fun things to take home. One lady talked to me as if I were the only one at the Y.

During the summer, I took diving lessons at Palisade Park. The first time I jumped off the board, I thought I would drown. I had to jump off the board several times before my coach convinced me that I would come up and wouldn't die. Diving was fun, although I felt alone, I went on a bus alone and didn't really have friends who went with me. But I did learn how to dive off of a diving board. I would talk to Judy out loud on the bus.

When Grandma and Aunt Mary came to Bloomfield, I knew it would be fun. We would go to New York City to the Ice Capades or the circus. Sometimes we went shopping, although I didn't ever buy another hat in New York. Mommy, Grandma, and Aunt Mary sometimes left us kids at home and went on game shows.

When I was in sixth grade, we took a class trip to New York in the spring. We went by bus to Radio City Music Hall and saw a movie called, *Please Don't Eat the Daisies*, starring Doris Day. Before we went on this trip, we had a manners class, as we were also going to a very nice restaurant to eat. We had to wear our best clothes and be on our best behavior.

Easter was near, and I wanted to wear Princess Ann heels, stockings, and a bra. Mommy said I wasn't ready; Daddy said I was. After much discussion, Daddy took me to buy the shoes, stockings, a mint-green suit, a pill-box hat to match the suit, a half-slip, and a bra. I walked around the house in my new outfit all week before the trip to New York. The hard part was walking in those shoes with a small heel.

Since Daddy was a flight engineer for TWA, we got discounted airline tickets. Our family went on our first real vacation to Disneyland and Knott's Berry Farm in California. When we flew into the airport, there were the largest jack rabbits on the runway. Through the plane window, I said, "Shoo, shoo, get off the runway." Daddy said at times they'd get in the plane engines and die.

Disneyland was overwhelming—the rides, Mickey Mouse, the shops, Adventure Land, Space Land. We stayed there for three days; it was hard to take it all in. Then we went to Knott's Berry Farm, which wasn't a farm at all. Some famous movies had been made there. My brother sat on the lap of statue of a western bar girl. It sure looked real. What an exciting time; it was a real vacation, just like the ones that my classmates talked about. Now I had my own adventure to talk about.

At times, Judy would show up; she always gave me comfort, especially when I had to walk home from the dentist's office alone. I did not mind going to the dentist, since it meant I would have time with Judy. She brought up subjects I was unsure about, like why we had to have mother-daughter talks at school and watch a movie on the same topic. I sure wasn't ready for that talk. The subject was never brought up again. Why did my mother's friend keep blood in a cooler in her car?

I felt lucky when Daddy and his friend took me on flights with them, especially when they made me an official junior airline stewardess. It was fun delivering coffee and then staying with my daddy in the cockpit.

Not long after that, Daddy got laid off from TWA. He did some odd jobs for other airlines, like flying monkeys from Africa to New York. The bathroom was in the back of the plane, where the monkeys were housed, and it was a long flight. So when he went to the bathroom, the monkeys would urinate on him. When he got home, Mommy made him shower outside and threw his clothes in the trashcan.

In January or February, he took a test for the Federal Aviation Agency, and then was stationed in Cincinnati, Ohio. He was alone out there for about five months, until we got out of school, and he had to find a home for us again. Mommy's instructions were that she didn't want to live in the country. Mommy didn't have a realtor license, but she did a good job of selling the house and packing things up to move us to Ohio.

I was ready to graduate from the sixth grade at Oakview Elementary School, Bloomfield —proper etiquette taught, dance classes in place, swimming and diving lessons complete. I graduated from my remedial classes in everything—math, reading, and writing—and received my official school banner, autograph book, and certificate. We were to move to Cincinnati in a short time.

New Jersey had introduced big changes; what would Ohio hold in store? What about the time in-between?

Hope is a journey, not a destination: journey with me, dear God.

Chapter 4
HOPE THROUGH THE DARKNESS

Before we moved from New Jersey to Ohio, I spent time in Peckville, at my parents' friends' house. They had the only bakery in town and showed me how they made donuts, hard rolls, and bread. The mixing bowls were huge, and magical; the right amount of sugar, flour, vanilla, and secret ingredients went into the huge bowls, and a delightful treat came out. Mixing and baking were done by 5:00 a.m.; the trucks left while the bread was hot out of the oven. The bakery smelled wonderful.

One experience that summer was not too magical. It was a warm summer's day. I was in the basement of their house on Main Street, when I was surprised to realize that their son was there. He was about five years older than I was. We had grown up together, and I didn't think too much of him.

I was standing near the large wash sink, folding the wash when he pinned me with bodily force against the sink and said, "If you tell your parents, I will deny it. If you scream, I'll cover your mouth."

The stairs were near, but just far enough away that I couldn't get to them. Things happened very quickly, and I felt pressure between my legs … and I can't remember the rest, or much about that afternoon.

I slept in the den, which was between the kitchen and the bedrooms. During the night, I felt the young man crawl into bed with me. I was too frightened to scream. He wiggled himself in the bed and said again, "If you tell your parents, I will deny it." I was twelve. I had no idea what had happened to me. I was quite naïve for a twelve-year-old.

I stuffed the incidents in my head and did not tell anyone. But I never went to the bakery or stayed at that house again. I made a point of staying at Baba's house. No one ever asked me why.

The house in Bloomfield was packed up by movers. I packed my dolls and the things I used for my pretend-school classes. My Girl Scout troop gave me a going-away party and a stuffed dog with all their best wishes on it. My piano teacher gave me a paper keyboard, so that I could practice without a piano. I'd learned the basics, but was not very serious about it. I never took lessons again.

Daddy had found a house not too far out of Cincinnati. Mommy called it the country; there were no stores we could walk to, and we had to drive everywhere and take a school bus to school. The house was a nice, new, brick ranch house in Milford, Ohio. It had a full basement, a bomb shelter, a cistern that provided water, and a lots of room for roller skating. When we first moved in, there was a two-car garage, which daddy turned into a large den with a fireplace.

Our neighbor had said we would have plenty of water as, in addition to the water from the cistern, water was delivered as well. Mommy was really mad. "What kind of house did your father get us, where water has to be delivered?" The day we moved in, I turned off the water from the cistern; I had no idea what it was. The neighbor came over and fixed the problem. I was banned from that part of the basement.

I went to Milford Elementary School, which had a section for the seventh graders. My teacher was Mr. Adams, and he was my ideal. The very first day of school, I got on the wrong bus to go home; I had no idea where I was going. When I didn't return home at the appropriate time, my mother called the school. Mr. Adams tracked me down; I was about fifteen minutes from the house. The bus driver was in a quandary; he realized I had just moved to Milford and had no idea where I was, so he stopped at the country store and called the school. Then he delivered me to my house personally.

Mr. Adams was a wonderful teacher; he must have read the school records, because I was elected, due to his lobbying, class secretary. Mr. Adams helped me with the secretary notes each month. Then I was voted best-dressed girl of the seventh grade. Wow. I tried so hard with my studies; for once, I had a teacher who believed in me. When I didn't understand something, he asked me to stay after school and reviewed the day's material with me.

I may have taken his kindness for granted. I was one of six girls who climbed out of the girls' bathroom window and skipped the music lesson. Mr. Adams lined us up in front of the class and hit the palm of our hands with a ruler. I think I was sorrier that I disappointed Mr. Adams than I was that I got in trouble. Remember this was 1960 in rural Ohio.

Mr. Adams took the class to the roller-skating rink. Boy, was I ever in my element. I now had had friends, and I helped them learn how to skate. My first real crush was on a set of twins, and they already knew how to skate. For Christmas that year, I got my own skates and carrying case. Every weekend I went to the skating rink.

Going to church was sometimes difficult as it was a good distance from the house. Because of the distance, I was not enrolled in religious education, and the family did not go to church regularly.

Mommy didn't like Ohio, so by mid-January, Daddy was looking for a job closer to Pennsylvania. One job was in Richmond, Virginia. Mommy, Daddy, and Robert drove there. Mommy came back to Ohio with a cup of red clay and said, "This is where we are moving."

My only birthday in Ohio was wonderful. I went on a local "American Bandstand"–type TV show. I met a young man; we danced the night away on TV, and then went to Bob's Big Boy for strawberry pie. It was just him and me and Daddy.

I was crushed when I found out we were moving to Virginia. Maybe it's a female thing, but my life was complete just holding hands, walking in the park, and sharing dreams that someday my true love would come.

Hope is a path that God sets for us, and we have no idea where it will lead.

CHAPTER 5
HOPE IN HOME

WE MOVED TO Highland Springs, Virginia, in July 1961. As we drove, we passed a moving van that had broken down on the side of the road. Daddy joked, "That could be our furniture." Well, it was no joke; that was our furniture. Daddy had found a house to rent, but because we did not have furniture, we slept in a boarding house the first couple of weeks. The bird and guinea pig stayed at the house.

My parents took us Saint John's Catholic Church in Highland Springs. There we met Father Donfred Stockert, the pastor. He spoke to my parents and then he helped us find a mattress from a furniture store so we could stay at the house.

I was not ready to be a Southern belle, which to me meant stuff called grits, red clay, no furniture, staying at a boarding house, sleeping on a mattress, having a pet guinea pig and a pet bird, changing my name to Mary, and no letters from the love of my life in Ohio.

The water tasted funny, so I wouldn't drink it. I even asked my grandparents to bring water from Pennsylvania when they came to visit. It felt like we were camping; the neighbors and people from the church brought us food and clean sheets. With no air conditioning, we hardly needed sheets. August in Virginia is hot and humid.

I wrote a letter to my love every day, but after a month of not hearing from him, I became depressed about the whole situation. Moving, no furniture, no friends, and to top it off, the dirt in our backyard was red, red clay. I found comfort in taking care of my guinea pig.

Mommy was now called Mama, as that's what the neighborhood children called their mother. She went to three different schools to register us; elementary school for Robert, junior high for me, and high school for Joe. Fairfield Middle School was a campus school and different from any school I had been to. The first day of school I met Sue at the bus stop; she showed me were to get off the bus and where my homeroom was. We met at the bus ramp to go home and she showed me which bus to get on. At least, that was better than Ohio.

In other areas I was on my own, and I didn't do well. I didn't look carefully; I just saw the sign that said restroom and, oops, I walked right into the boys' bathroom. I was so embarrassed that I ran right back out and ran down a long sidewalk, hoping no one saw me. I dashed into my next class and sat there, hoping I wouldn't see anyone from the bathroom. Thank God, I didn't.

When the next bell rang, I wanted to hustle to the next class, but I did not know where it was. That first day I asked so many students for directions. I was lost in sea of students. When I got home, I told Daddy I hated that school and wanted to go back to Ohio. In the welcome packet, Daddy found a map of the campus. He and I took the map and navigated the schedule of my classes.

The next day went smoother, except the language was peculiar to me. The teachers slurred some of the words together. Every time a student didn't understand a teacher, he or she said, "sir," "ma'am," "yes sir" or "no ma'am." In the other states I had lived in, we said yes or no, and that was all.

My eighth-grade English teacher asked me to read the blackboard. When I couldn't, she had me move up a couple of seats. When I still couldn't read the blackboard, she asked me to move up again. Finally she called my parents. Daddy took me to an eye doctor in Richmond, and the teacher was right: I couldn't see. I got my first pair of glasses. When I left the eye doctor with my new glasses, the colors looked brighter, the stop signs were a bright red, and the trees were bright green. A new world appeared.

Art became one of my favorite classes. The colors seemed to pop of the canvas, and I used a lot of bright colors; red, orange and yellow became my favorite colors. Using and mixing colors was my favorite new project. I used art to distract me from my dislike of Virginia; through art, some of the depression lifted.

I was always getting grounded by my parents for something. That meant no going out and no phone. Most of the time it wasn't too bad, as Sue got grounded by my parents too. She was allowed to come to the house, but we could not go anywhere. In Henrico County in the early 1960s, you were allowed to drive at age fifteen and a half, but only in the county, so when we were able to get out, Sue drove me and our friends around in her 1957 blue-and-white Ford Fairlane.

We stayed within the county borders, until one hot summer day when we ventured beyond to visit some of her relatives in a nearby county. On the way back, we went skinny dipping in Kent Lake. We got out of the water and then worried about being seen. Luckily for us, Sue had a blanket in the trunk. When I got home, my parents were asleep, and I quietly took a shower and went to bed. It was thrilling to have such an experience of my own.

I liked Highland Springs High School. I loved art and often stayed after school to finish a project. The library club interested me, and I volunteered twice a week to put magazines and newspapers in chronological order.

Speech class was a new experience. Different kinds of speeches fascinated me. Changing the subject matter and preparing the speech captured my creative thinking. Mom told me about a speech she gave when she was in school; it was on how to make Jell-O. I tried that and it worked; it wasn't too creative, but my grade was good. We gave speeches on what we wanted to be. I wanted to be a flight attendant for TWA. The day of the speech I spoke as if I already were a stewardess. Another time, we had to give exact directions to where we lived. I had practiced this speech with my daddy since I was a little girl in Bloomfield; north, south, east, and west were parts of a pilot's navigational tools. I learned how to read a map while learning the states and capitals and some of the airport abbreviations when my daddy flew out of Idlewild, LaGuardia, and Newark. I was feeling more at home.

I wasn't sure if I was flirty or just flighty, but I tried out for the girls basketball team, only because the boys football team practiced at the same time. I had no clue how to play basketball, but it was good to walk home after practice hand in hand with my new neighbor and boyfriend. I got cut from the team, but he got to play football.

Some Sundays I told my family I was going to early Mass and wanted to walk the two miles to church to be with God. Actually, I wanted to walk past another Mr. Wonderful's house. He played the guitar and would sing to me. He'd pick me up at the bus stop, and we'd head for the park. I liked going to church, but boys held a greater attraction than the Eucharist.

I enjoyed being in the Catholic Youth Organization (CYO) and participating in activities such as camping, horse riding, and going to the mountains and the beach. Just being around other Catholic youths helped my self-esteem, which seemed to be affected by their self-esteem. In tenth grade, the CYO staged *The Song of Bernadette*. How exciting it was to be in a play in which Bernadette saw a vision of the Blessed Mother. There were so many practices, scene by scene, line by line. There was a cast of over twenty members, and Father Stockert directed the play. It was a wonderful experience, although I played a small part, Jean Abadie, Bernadette's friend.

I was secretary of the CYO. Father Stockert took us swimming in the winter at the Cavalier Hotel in Hampton, Virginia. On the way home, we stopped at a nice restaurant. Father ordered a beer, and I couldn't believe it, a priest drinking a beer. With my loud voice, I yelled, "Father's drinking a beer." He took us camping, horseback riding, and to the mountains. We always had Mass in the morning, and the girls had to wear skirts and the boys, long pants.

My circle of friends was growing, and I didn't know how to balance the teenage time and the who-was-I time. I didn't want to hurt people along the way. I met a lifetime friend, and she and her family became close to me. Dianne was my church friend and brought me into a new circle of friends at school. She hung out with a band named the Barracudas. Dianne and I became their groupies. One of the members went to our church; in fact, a lot of our church friends became our secular friends.

During church activities, Father asked us to be part of the liturgy. We had to take up the offering or do the readings. Some of my friends were altar boys. This was hard on Sue, my best friend; she didn't go to church, although I tried very hard to get her to go. She sometimes drove me and waited in the car. I felt so sorry she could not participate in my new activities with the CYO.

We did join a sorority together. Kappa Beta Gamma. We went through the rush together doing stupid things, like sucking a baby pacifier in public, carrying someone's books, and being blindfolded in the shower at school. We had formal teas to raise money for the poor, but I didn't see why we would act crazy to then do good. I could not find the purpose.

Mama went to the doctor as she thought she had the flu; it was a flu named David. My parents were forty-one and forty-two when David was born; he brought quite a change to the household. Joe, my oldest brother, was going to Richmond Polytechnic Institute, now known as Virginia Commonwealth University, and then along came David. At times, I made Mama mad by telling her she'd been bit by a trouser worm, and it got infected. She was sick during most of the pregnancy and wasn't in any mood to be teased.

On May 2, 1963, David became the king of the household, as Grandma Budjinski would say. He was baptized in Olyphant, Pennsylvania, as there was no Byzantine-rite Catholic church in Richmond. There was a big party at Baba's house for David's baptism.

Each afternoon, after school I would take David for walks—first in the stroller and then in the wagon. He liked the wagon best. I was fifteen when David was born and I learned a lot about babies and how to take care of them.

Hope is for things unseen.

CHAPTER 6
HOPE IN MEANINGFUL ACTIVITY

BREAKING INTO THE working world was a challenge. After an interview at the local department store, an elderly lady looked at me and said, "Honey, I'm Polish, and I like your spunk, but you have to be sixteen to work or get a work permit from the county." I applied for a work permit and received it. One downside of the job was that I didn't drive yet, and my parents had to take me back and forth from work. Another downside was that I didn't know how to count change, so until I learn to do so, I worked in the jewelry department, organizing the jewelry and cleaning the glass cases.

The lady who hired me taught me how to make change, and she practiced with me every day. I worked every Sunday morning so it seemed my church life would slip away, unless I went to the 7:00 a.m. Mass and walked to church. Robert was now an altar boy, and my parents went to the Mass at which he served.

When I wasn't working, I was babysitting. Now that was an experience, as I spent more money on the three children—a five-year-old boy, a three-year-old girl, and a baby boy about six months old—than I made babysitting. It was like playing house. The children needed a lot—baths, clean sheets, clean clothes, food. Each time I sat for them, I took clothes I purchased at my job. I made them stockings at Christmas.

Mom and Dad invited a foreign exchange student to our home, an American Field Student (AFS). Gabi was Jewish and had requested to be with a Catholic family. One night I thought I was in another country. A local rabbi asked Gabi come to dinner; the Jewish community was going to have a party for him. Gabi would not accept unless I went with him.

We went to the rabbi's home and there were so many pieces of silver ware on the table, I had no idea which one to use first. I looked at Gabi, and he said, "Just do what they do." After dinner, one of the children performed a piano concert. Waiting for the words, I realized there were no words, just music. How strange this house was: a maid who didn't smile, a song with no words, and a language I'd never heard before. Gabi translated for me, as Hebrew was his native language. Later, we went to a party for the teenagers. We sang and danced and socialized. That night, I discovered a whole different world just a short drive from my home.

Mama, Gabi, me, and Robert.

In 1964, Highland Springs High School accepted what my parents called two "colored" people. At first I was curious, as I had never seen a black person up close before. I wondered if they believed in the same God I believed in. It wasn't long before I became friends with the teenage girl, Jane, who was in one of my classes. She was bused in from another part of town.

Her parents would not allow her to come to my house, so we met in the library. Sometimes she ate alone and that really bothered me, so I would invite her to my lunch table. Some of the other teenagers would get up and leave the table. That hurt my feelings. Jane told me she wasn't allowed to use the same bathroom I used or drink out of the same water fountain, and she rode in the back of the bus. When her family went out to eat, they went to the backdoor and sat in a different part of restaurant.

My dad took me fishing at the Chickahominy River, and on the way there we saw a sign in front of a rundown restaurant: "Colored only." While we fished, Daddy and I had a long talk about segregation and prejudice. Daddy had started to teach Sunday school at Saint John's. On these fishing trips, he tried out his lessons on me. We talked about life; at times he would add some humor, and at times I felt trapped and just listened to what was on his mind.

Once he said, "Maryalyce, a woman can run faster with her dress up than a man can run with his pants down." Later I learned what that was supposed to mean. Daddy was trying to protect me from "parking" on a car date in the dummy town. During World War II, the army had built a dummy town near Byrd Airport as a decoy, hoping it would get hit first if Richmond came under attack. The dummy town had paved streets, fire hydrants, street lights, and buildings made from scrap material. By the 1960s, this place was a hangout for teenagers and John Law. My friend always said that she'd seen John Law. I wondered who John Law was until someone explained that was another name for the local police.

Sue's parents had a cottage in Matthews, Virginia. We went down there often. She went to the Matthews High School prom, and I met this guy whose parents owned fleet of dump trucks. Several times he came by the house in this huge dump truck. The truck was clean and he was a nice guy, but my parents did not like having a dump truck parked in the front of our house or for that to be the vehicle in which I'd go out in on a date. The relationship didn't last long, but it was fun while it lasted.

Some things you can be taught; some you have to learn for yourself; others can only be experienced.

Hope is for teenagers.

CHAPTER 7
HOPE IN TRANSITIONS

SWEET SIXTEEN. A well-prepared surprise was planned for my sixteenth birthday. Mama and Daddy took me to Nick's for dinner, while my CYO friends set up a party at the church social hall. I was totally surprised. There was so much food, dancing, and good clean fun, and Daddy filmed everything with a movie camera.

Father Stockert invited a few of us to the beach for a weekend. We met one of his nieces, who was going into the convent. We had prayer and Mass on the beach each day.

As I was now sixteen, my hours increased at work: long lines of shoppers before Christmas; two days of inventory, counting and recounting, after the holiday; long hours at weekends; and that pink smock with Zayer written on it. The store manager's son was about my age, and I kind of liked him. School and work were all I did, so it was a natural thing to meet him in the break room; that was as far as that went.

My studies, my social life, and church life faltered all at once. I applied for a job at a grocery store that was closer to the house; it would make it easier for my parents to transport me to and from work.

I met a boy who went to Varina High School. His parents were deaf, and he communicated with them using sign language. I learned a little myself. He was very nice to me. He was a year older and joined the navy after graduation. He asked me to take his parents to see him at his ship, the USS *Forrestal*, which was docked in Norfolk. I picked them up and drove them to Norfolk; it was the quietest sixty miles I've ever driven.

We went on a day trip to the *Forrestal*. It was exciting to be on an aircraft carrier with jets that flew off the deck. We got to see some take offs and landings. We ended the day watching a beautiful sunset from the ship.

We wrote to each other for a while; then Mama had a talk with me about having deaf children. She suggested that I not see him anymore; besides, he wasn't Catholic. But my friend Sue helped me go see him. She'd park the car a block away from my house. I'd jump out of the bathroom window and onto the outdoor freezer; then I'd would meet her at the car. We'd would push the car a little and start it. We did the same when I returned home in the early morning. The relationship did not last, but I got pretty good at this new escape method, which was convenient when we went out at night.

Studying during junior year wasn't my primary objective. I liked geography and did well in it; after all, I needed it to become a stewardess. Speech was my best subject; I got with As and Bs. One semester struggling with French convinced me that I no longer wanted to fly overseas. In English, I got consistent Cs or Ds, and basic math was Cs, home economics was As and Bs. I enjoyed school and missed very little.

I had my tonsils out between my junior and senior years, but I was out of commission from work for longer than expected because I got the mumps while in the hospital. During the summer, I took my driving test—twice. Daddy went with me the first time, and I failed the written test. A week later, Mama took me, and I passed with no problem.

Joe, my oldest brother, was due to come home from Vietnam. My parents bought another house in Highland Springs, so there would be room for him. Daddy was good at fixing houses up.

During my senior year, I entered the Junior Miss Virginia Pageant.

I made my suit, an olive-green, corduroy, two-piece lined in light-green rayon. Mama found a brown handbag and shoes to match. The judges met the contestants at a tea; it was about poise, social skills, posture, and answering questions from all the judges. We had to present a talent. I thought mine was speech, so I made up a skit about a girl named Little Audrey who didn't know how to say "Mary Had a Little Lamb." I put ribbons in my hair, wore a childlike dress, and Mary Jane shoes.

Little Audrey goes to her mother, but she was baking. Her father was typing, her brother was reading, and her sister was cheering. For each of them, she repeated, with gestures: "Mary had a little lamb, two eggs, whose flees was white as snow, Ding, everywhere that Mary went, flip a page of the book, the lamb was sure to go, with a cheer."

Four weeks and many practices later, I was alone on the stage of Highland Springs High School, doing my little skit. After the talent portion, we lined up in long gowns; mine, $2 from a garage sale at the Sacred Heart Cathedral downtown, was pink and flowing, the most beautiful dress I'd ever seen. A judge asked each one of us a question. I was so nervous I can remember neither my question nor my answer. We returned to the stage so the judges could announce the winner. Well, I wasn't third-, second, or first-runner up, and when they said "Mary," my right foot went out. I wanted to believe it was me, and my body tensed up, but it was another Mary who won the contest.

What a great experience! My parents and brothers were there; Father Stockert was there. We got a lot of prizes and a great experience. After the party, the person who did the curtain cues and lighting escorted me to a party at the home of one of the judge's. Sue saw me backstage; she knew how much courage it took for me to be on that stage. I was glad she came.

At that point, my life was all about passing and graduating. I had my heart set on being a stewardess. One of our neighbors was a teacher, and she tutored me in English and government. I still worked at the grocery store part-time. I dated one of the stock boys. We went to see Peter Paul, and Mary, a folk group I really liked. He took me to see wrestling, which I liked until I found out it was fake. He was a nice

Catholic guy, a bit older than I was, with nice family. My parents liked him, but my focus was on being a stewardess.

Father Stockert invited me to speak at the crowning of Mary in the May procession at church. I rehearsed my lines and was a little nervous. Mama bought me a new dress that had a hoop under it—right out of *Gone with the Wind*. We walked from the front to the side of the church, and just as I was about to go to the microphone, a gust of wind took that hoop over my head. I was so embarrassed I was barely able to say the prayer before the Blessed Mary. I wanted to hide, to be anywhere but where I was.

I went to my senior prom and wore the pink dress from the Junior Miss Virginia Pageant. My date was impatient, and we didn't stay at the prom but ended up in this dingy place in the Fan district. Needless to say, I didn't have a good time.

The baccalaureate in June 1966 was held at Bailey Field, the school's athletic field. Graduation was to follow immediately afterward at the same field. But rain was coming, and the graduation was moved to the Richmond Arena, near the Parker Field baseball diamond (now the home to the Flying Squirrels baseball team). As our names were called, we walked across the stage to get our diplomas. Some of my classmates cried; some had tears of joy for having made it through the ordeal. I was just glad to get it over with. I did not having a clue what was next, but it had to be better than high school.

I had saved enough money to purchase a new Volkswagen. The salesman taught me to use a stick shift; he had a lot of patience. Soon afterward, I was with a friend in front of Medical College of Virginia, and we got stuck on a very steep hill. I couldn't get the car to move forward or backward, and I was paralyzed. A Richmond Police officer helped me to get to flat land, and I never drove on that hill again.

Dianne and I made several trips to Virginia Beach; we went to the Peppermint Lounge and stayed in a rooming house with a lumpy bed. She enjoyed dancing and meeting sailors. We always returned home dead broke, with just enough money to get back through the Hampton Roads Tunnel.

I met a sailor, an American Indian from Oklahoma. He'd take the bus from Norfolk to visit me, and several times I took him home for dinner. Mama said he lived a long way away, and I should not get attached to him. One day she took me shopping, and I did not get back in time to pick him up from the bus station. I never saw him again, even though I looked for him whenever I went to the beach.

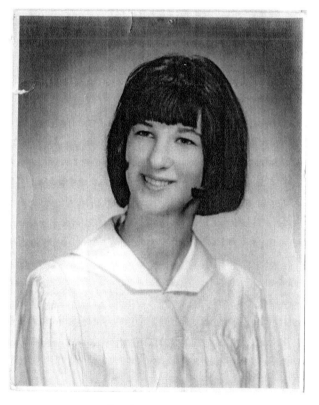

Graduation, 1966.

I have unanswered hopes and dreams.

CHAPTER 8
HOPE IN COMMITMENT

AT THE END of June 1966, I went to work for the Bank of Virginia in the downtown office at 8th and Main. My job was to prepare checks to go out with statements. I took several classes at the American Institute of Banking. The banking world probably was not for me. I found it hard to adjust to driving to work, doing the same thing day after day, people in the office not talking to each other, punching a clock, asking for breaks to go to the bathroom, paying for a parking space, and then walking in heels ten blocks to not be late. Then I went home to parents who wanted me do things I didn't do before, like pay rent and wash and buy my own clothes.

I went to the Virginia State Fair with someone named Larry. It was nice, holding hands, riding rides, sneaking into tents, laughing a lot. Several weeks later we went with some friends to a party in the Fan district. As we went upstairs, people were coming down. The Richmond police came and arrested us for disturbing the peace. We tried to explain that we'd just arrived, but they wouldn't listen. We were there; we seemed to be guilty. We were put in a paddy wagon and taken to the Richmond jail. It was terrible—a cell with a hole in the ground for a toilet. I cried until I couldn't cry any longer.

Larry had enough money to bail us all out, and we walked the twenty-five city blocks back to the car. I spent the night at a girlfriend's house. The next morning I went home. Larry went with me, and we explained what happened to my parents. My dad said, "You made your bed. Now you must lie in it."

I took all my savings out of the bank before we went to court on Monday morning. We lined up in front of the judge. Because I was so nervous I couldn't remember whether or not I was guilty, so I just said, "I didn't do it." The case was dismissed, and the judge said, "Next time you have a party, invite the man who said you were disturbing the peace." Life was going a little too fast.

I cashed my checks at Safeway and started dating a guy who worked there. He was two years younger than I was. He gave me a diamond ring; my parents made me give it back.

I started a job at the company where Joe worked. It designed cameras for NASA space projects. I met a man that worked there. When my dad found out Eric had two small children, was not Catholic, and was sweeping me of my feet, he wanted it not to be true, but it was. At that time in my life, I seemed to get God and men mixed up.

I believed everything Eric told me—that he loved me; that he wanted me to meet his children, who lived with his parents in Fredericksburg; and that he had a vacuum cleaner. I'd never dated someone who had his own apartment and his own vacuum cleaner. My parents took the telephone out of my bedroom. I would sneak downstairs to call him. "They will understand," he said.

Thirty days into the relationship, Eric asked me to make a choice—my family or him. He said he loved me so many times that I believed him. We played songs that confused me: were they about loving him or loving God? My father told the company where I'd met Eric to fire me, and I went to work for AT&T.

Each day I put clothes in my purse, and Eric picked me up from work and took me to his apartment. My parents forbid me to talk to him. Once he came to the house and tried to talk to my father. My father said that if he ever put foot on the property, he would have him arrested for trespassing.

Daddy took me to Virginia Beach to see Father Stockert, who had been transferred. Father Stockert wanted me to say that I would stop seeing Eric or would at least see him as a brother and stop having an intimate relationship. After two hours of talking and crying, I was unable to promise anything. I just wanted to go home and talk to Eric.

Eric made arrangements for us to be married on February 9, 1968, at the Dillon, South Carolina, Court House. I left the house and met Eric at his apartment. I called in sick to work, saying I had the flu. We left for Dillon on a cold sunny day. In the middle of the day, my supervisor went to my parents' home and to see how sick I was. My parents put two and two together and realized we had eloped.

Jamie 1ˢᵗ Communion with brother Joshua

I didn't hear from my parents until Daddy's birthday in March. I went to their house, told them I loved them, and gave Daddy a birthday present. My parents asked if I wanted the marriage annulled and whether I was pregnant, and I said no to both. I told to my younger brother David that I loved him very much and would always be there for him. He was only five years old; all he understood was that I was not home.

Every weekend, we went to see Eric's children, Jamie and Joshua, at his mother's house. We went to Mass together as a family, although I did not go to Communion, which was painful. I had no idea that separation from the Eucharist would have such an impact on me. I loved Jesus, and I could not have him.

Eric's children started to call me Mama; what a nice feeling! I felt like Maria in *The Sound of Music*, except the children's real mother was still alive. They did not see her, however. On Ash Wednesday we went to Saint Patrick's in the Church Hill section of Richmond. The priest said I could receive ashes, and I did. I was sure that would bring me to Communion again. Eric and I looked for a house within our price range, a good place to raise the children. We found one in North Side Richmond for $19,000, within our price range. It was a nice, brick, ranch, with three bedrooms, den, kitchen, one-and-a-half baths, living room, porch, and a shed where Eric could lift weights and tinker with a motorcycle he was building.

Eric wanted me to be a stay-at-home mom, so I quit my job at AT&T and settled into keeping house. Jamie and Josh came to live with us in June after school let out in Fredericksburg. Josh had one year before he would start to school, and Jamie was in second grade.

I taught them to pray before meals and at bedtime. Both children had some idea about how to pray as they attended a Baptist church in Fredericksburg with their grandmother. I took them to a well-recommended pediatrician to get immunizations for school. The doctor sat with me and said, "Do you have any idea what you are about to embark on? You are only nineteen years old. As those children grow they will want to know their real mother, and this will cause you pain."

I had no idea how to cook. Eric had to teach me how to boil water, make macaroni and cheese, and eventually make a meal. My Betty Crocker cookbook was a lifesaver. Right before school started, I called the pediatrician in a panic; something was wrong with Josh. He had an erection, but he was only five years old. The doctor calmed me down and said that was normal and I had a lot to learn about little boys. Then he laughed with me.

We wanted more children, and I found out I was about a month and a half pregnant. I had been to the doctor, and he confirmed it. I was so happy, I started wearing maternity clothes. I had morning sickness, afternoon sickness, and evening sickness.

It was on a Monday; that was when I did wash. I picked up the laundry basket; suddenly pain went through my stomach. I called the doctor; I had lost the baby. The doctor did a D&C, and within a week I was as good as new and ready to try again

I spent my days hoping to have children.

CHAPTER 9
HOPE IN THE KINDNESS OF STRANGERS

I WENT TO see the priest at Our Lady of Lourdes; in fact, I saw five priests. They either left the priesthood or died, and I had to start all over, explaining my desire to return to the church and receive Communion. I had both children baptized in the Catholic faith; we had a big party and my whole family came, but I still could not receive Communion. Jamie was preparing for her First Communion. I made her dress and veil. I was raising them to practice a faith from which I was excluded.

I met with a priest at the cathedral, and he came to the house several times. He also met with my parents. I told him how much I missed going to Communion and receiving Jesus, how much I loved God. There was an informal hearing, and the result was that I could partake in all aspects of the Catholic Church. The first thing I did was go to confession. All I could do was cry, I was so happy. I felt like I was floating on air as I went to Communion that Sunday.

In July, I was sick and losing weight. I went to the doctor and found out I was going to have a baby. As before, I had morning sickness and evening sickness. Fixing meals and taking care of the children became difficult. I tried to work part-time at a gift store to make extra money for Christmas, but I could only manage three hours. Then I'd go home and take a nap until the children came home from school and it was time to fix dinner. The sofa and I became friends.

Eric changed jobs and worked part-time a couple of nights a week. I would pull myself together long enough to get dinner and help the children with their homework and baths. I tried hard not to let them see how sick I was. I motivated myself to lead a Girl Scout troop one day a week and a Cub Scout den on another day. All I wanted on Friday night was to go out for pizza with Eric and the children, which became a tradition.

That is until the night of February 3, when the pains came fast and hard. They stopped by morning, but Eric took me to the doctor's office. The doctor sent me home and told me to stay in bed. The next day I went back to the doctor; although the baby was not due until March, the pain was back. Eric took me to Medical College of Virginia Hospital, and that evening Robert Anthony was born—a mere three pounds, two ounces. My parents were in the waiting room.

Doctors decided that Robert Anthony needed to be in a special hospital for premature babies. When they took the baby, my daddy went too and baptized Robert Anthony in the elevator. Eric and my RH factors were different; Eric's was positive, and mine was negative.

Robert Anthony had difficulty breathing. Eric called to tell me that the baby did not make it through the night. I did not believe him. The nurse came in with something to calm me down; she said it had to do with our blood being different. She said that what I had was called a legal abortion, because I'd gone into early labor. I was angry. I'd never heard of a legal abortion; this nurse had made a mistake. Not ever seeing my baby boy with a name attached to him kept me sad all the time.

Eric arranged to bury Robert Anthony at Signal Hill Memorial Park. He had purchased two plots, and the baby was buried at the foot of one of them. The nurse pushed me in a wheelchair out of the hospital; I left with no baby and empty dreams,.

I put the baby things away on a day I was by myself, folding them neatly and putting them in a box marked "baby things." September came, both children were in school. I got a part-time job at Richmond Engineering Company, typing expense checks and doing jobs around the office. I even went to the bank each day. My hours were 9:00 a.m. to 1:00 p.m., five days a week. I continued with Scouting. Eric and I did some camping on the Ty River; with the extra money I made, I bought an old Jeep pickup for him to rebuild.

I started getting morning sickness, so the office moved my desk nearer to the bathroom. Yes, I was pregnant again. I was not quite as happy as I had been before. I decided to change doctors, as my friend Sue told me about a doctor who had just gotten out of the army and started a obstetric practice. I quit my job around Christmas, and the new doctor inserted a pessary to hold the baby in proper position. I was ordered to stay in bed and off my feet. My mother came over and fixed a week's worth of meals; all I had to do was put them in the oven. I was so grateful. In the mornings, Jamie helped Josh get ready for school. I only did laundry when my mother came over. I felt nauseous all the time. I gained weight, but slowly. Eric brought home milkshakes, hoping they would help me put on some weight.

In February 1971, a lady came to our door soliciting for the Heart Fund. She said she lived a block away; she was Catholic, had three boys, and she was from Sugar Notch, Pennsylvania, just a few towns from where I'd been baptized. She solicited for the Heart Fund each year. Her name was Janice, and I invited her in for tea. Janice would come down and check on me regularly.

When she came on February 27, I wasn't home. Eric had taken me to the hospital as my water broke during the night. The doctor met us at the hospital; he tried to stop the labor. The pains stopped, but he would not release me, I was moved to a regular room for observation. For a while, we thought things were going well.

On February 29, I gave birth to a beautiful red-headed baby boy with long fingers and toes. Eric stayed with me during the delivery. Coming off the epidural, I was shaking and so cold; the nurse said that was normal. In the recovery room, I was warm and felt good inside. The pediatrician came in and said the baby was doing okay. We figured since he was conceived on the Ty River, we would call him Ty Wayne; actually I'd wanted to call him John Wayne, after my doctor.

The next morning the doctor told me Ty had not made it through the night. He had died of hyaline membrane disease, the same thing Robert Anthony had died from. The doctor, filled with his care and compassion, had me taken to a private room. I asked for the funeral to be postponed until I was able to go. I went to the funeral of my baby boy, who is buried next to his brother.

Coming home was much different this time. My new friend Janice put the baby clothes away and had the crib taken down before I got there. She met me at the door with tea and flowers.

I keep hoping for things unseen.

CHAPTER 10
HOPE THROUGH DESPAIR

I CRIED UNTIL I could cry no longer. Eric encouraged me to find a job, but all I could do was cry and fall deeper into a pit of depression. In addition, I had to be home when the children got home from school. My options were limited.

I found a job at a restaurant a couple of miles away, where I worked the breakfast shift. One Monday, my boss came and told me the restaurant was going topless, but if I wanted to stay, I could. I told him no.

Two weeks later, I was working 8:00 a.m. to 2:00 p.m. at Richmond Memorial Hospital Credit Union. I liked the job, and I liked that people who belonged to a credit union were called members. This job was personable because the membership was small. Eric was now working at General Electric from 3:00 p.m. to 11:00 p.m., so that left me to juggle Girl Scouts, Cub Scouts, and church activities with the children.

Eric brought in a box and put it on the kitchen counter. It was the latest thing in cooking—a microwave. I had seen the pros and cons on TV, and Eric's father was sure it wasn't good for the environment, so I used the expensive thing to boil water and warm up food.

Janice was going to have a baby; going to the shower was hard, but I went because I liked her. Janice's baby, Dominic, died the first week

47

in December. She said to me she could now walk this path with me, as she'd come home as empty as I had.

As a leader with the Girl Scouts, I went camping twice a year, mostly at Pocahontas State Park in Chesterfield. I needed another person to accompany me, so Susie, who worked an office next door at the hospital, agreed to go. She and I stayed in the leader's cabin. When we were getting ready for bed, Sue took off her shirt and bra, and I was horrified—her breasts were not white. Susie was African American, and because I was not around black people, I thought for sure her breasts would be white. She got a big laugh out of my ignorance.

A local Jeep dealership formed a four-wheel-drive club. It took time to get this club to come together. At first I thought it was a beer-drinking club, but as we got to know each other, we decided that it would be a family-oriented group with camping and fellowship. I became the first secretary, which exposed all my writing flaws. I put a newsletter together; someone else edited it. We met once a month; the group grew. We had a lot of family fun. One event was a blindfold race on a course. The wife or female friend was blindfolded, and the opposite sex told her how to drive the course. We went on trail rides in the George Washington National Park and cleared trails too, with the help of rangers. The wives in the club bonded, and I now had some new friends. Eric still worked evening shift.

Josh and Jamie took karate. Jamie was also was on the gymnastic team, and Josh played football. Sometimes I felt more like a taxi driver than a mom. During the summer, Janice, her three boys, and my two took day trips to Virginia Beach. We'd get some chicken and fixings and pack a cooler of drinks, and I'd drive her big station wagon to the beach. We had fun and talked about private secrets, while the children played on the beach. We took a detour one day and went to the National Sea Shore Park. Josh walked into a hornets', nest, and we spent most of that day at the hospital.

I left the credit union and joined the staff at the hospital pharmacy. I took a few classes taught by the pharmacy staff. I primarily did paper work, but sometimes I delivered medications to the wards. When I found out a grocery store was paying the cashiers $1.50 more than I was getting at the hospital, I applied and got the job. I worked first as a cashier and then in most of the other departments. I worked part-time but was asked a number of times to work full-time as a department manager. Each time I turned the offer down, as Eric wanted me to be with the children in the evening. After a couple of years, Janice started working at the store, also part-time.

Jamie and Josh were both active in sports. I started to learn karate as well, as I got tired of just watching. The three of us competed in tournaments and self-defense demonstrations. Jamie became very competitive in gymnastics and was on the middle-school gymnastic team.

I was pregnant again, but I lost the baby after a month. The doctor did a D&C and recommended that I have a hysterectomy. My uterus could not hold a baby up to full-term; it appeared to be tilted. The pain of losing another baby was too hard to bear. Still, it was a hard discussion. Daddy got upset, as he was afraid that if I tried again, I might die in the process. Eric and my father talked me into having the operation; I was only twenty-six years old. At that time, the operation could not be done in a Catholic hospital, so it was done where I'd worked at the credit union.

I was sure I was giving something up; I was not ready to seek another plan in my life.

I hope God knows my struggle.

Chapter 11
HOPE IN CHANGE

ERIC STARTED ACTING weird; he would bring home friends from work after midnight, when the children and I were asleep. Sometimes these gatherings became full-blown parties, with loud music, pot-smoking, and loud voices. Eric bought an expensive stereo, although we could have used the money to purchase Christmas presents for the children. I tried to be understanding, as most of the women and men were on his crew. When they didn't meet at the house, they all met a truck stop, and Eric would not come home till morning. I started losing both sleep and weight.

My job changed; although it was still part-time, it was at a new store, twenty minutes away. I told my doctor about my growing depression; he suggested I see a psychiatrist as the stress of raising two preteenagers by myself was difficult.

Jamie found a kitten in a drainpipe near our house. She named her Missy Kitty, who was about twelve weeks old when she ran out in front of a car and got wrapped up in the front grill. She made her way to the backyard and hid under the porch; after much coaxing, Jamie and I got her out. We took her to the veterinarian; the skin on her leg had been peeled back like a banana. The veterinarian sewed the skin together, and we brought the kitten home. Jamie kept the kitten in her room and nursed her back to health.

We had planned a trip to Fredericksburg for a weekend, so Jamie made a safe place for Miss Kitty from Saturday morning to Sunday afternoon. When we returned, Jamie's room smelled terrible; gangrene had set in. We returned to the veterinarian, and he gave us two choices: try to save the kitten and take the leg off up to the shoulder, or put the kitten to sleep. Jamie took the choices to her father, who said, "Put the kitten to sleep." I said, "Let's try and save her." I went back to the veterinarian, who said that if Jamie and I came by twice a day to feed and give the kitten medication, he would not charge us. He operated on Missy Kitty, and each morning, before work, I went to the vet's office to feed and give medication to the kitten. Jamie went with me in the evening. Miss Kitty now had a new name, Tripod. Our veterinarian was so compassionate and loved animals so much, he let us come from November to January and never charged us. He said that Tripod survived because we were there each day.

The Old Dominion Four-Wheel Drive Club was sponsoring members to do the March of Dime Walk America, a twenty-three-mile walk through Richmond. Someone who was dating one of my friends encouraged me to do the walk; since I had been doing some training in karate, I signed up. At each checkpoint I was tempted to quit, but each checkpoint also had friends from the club cheering me on. I completed the walk, and donations from sponsors amounted to over $100. When I got home, I soaked my body for hours; every bone in my body hurt, especially my feet.

The Old Dominion Club made an agreement with a land owner in Cumberland County to build a four-wheeler motor-cross racing track. Eric, the owner, and several men from the club designed it. Eric had done some four-wheel-drive racing in Pennsylvania and came home with a several trophies. Our whole family spent many weekends clearing the track. We referred to the track as Bodacious. The club was taking a different turn.

During this time, I was meeting with a therapist. Eric met with her once; after that one meeting the therapist told me to prepare myself: Eric would leave me soon. I didn't believe her. I didn't want to believe her.

One day, I left work and went home for lunch; I never had lunch. A female friend of Eric's was leaving our street. When I went into the house, we had an argument about the time he was spending with her. I grabbed his shirt, and I ended up on the floor next to the refrigerator. I could not get up, not because of any physical injury but because of emotional exhaustion.

I decided to check myself into the hospital, as my therapist suggested. Janice agreed to take care of the children until I came home. Eric drove me to the hospital, and that is where he left me—at the doors of Westbrook Hospital on April 5, 1976.

The first two days I just slept, as I had not had a full night's sleep in months. The nurses walked me to and from meals. I was too depressed to eat. I was not hungry. It was a week or so before my appetite came back. Eric came to visit just once and that was so I could sign income tax papers. I asked for the priest, but they said he might interfere with my therapy.

I felt like I had died—no priest, no husband, and someone else was looking after the children. I was only half alive. I put a tombstone on my door, labeled "Supermom died." I painted a picture of just half a face. I learned a lot about myself in the hospital. I learned that I was a good person. I wanted to see my children. I got weekend passes to go home.

The first time I went home, Eric, the cookbook, a few pictures, and most of his clothes were all gone. He was gone, and I didn't know where.

Jamie and Josh stayed with me when I left the hospital for good. We stayed at the house. I went back to work part-time for the grocery store, but I needed a full time job. Some of the men in the four-wheel-drive club told me about a job opening in the reprint department of a printing company. I filled out an application, as I had some knowledge about art from high school.

Mr. Rose interviewed me and reviewed my application. I told him I was going through a divorce and getting help for situational depression, and I needed a full-time job to take care of the children. He answered that anyone willing to be that honest was the person he should hire. I started work on July 6, 1976.

My therapist and I worked on whether the children should stay with me or with their father. He would come by every couple of weeks and take them out for a while. The children told me where he lived and that the woman he worked with lived a couple of houses away from him. The therapist said it would be best if the children made up their own minds about where to live.

Eventually, Josh left and moved in with his father, and Jamie stayed with me. The words their first pediatrician had said haunted me: "They'll say, 'You're not my mother and I can do what I want.'" Although it was painful, I let him make his own choice.

I tried to keep the children together; every Wednesday we went out to supper. But Jamie and Josh eventually spent less and less time with each other. Jamie made the Henrico High School gymnastics team, and I enjoyed watching and cheering her on. I started attending a program for offset printing at Richmond Technical School one night a week.

The next year, I was encouraged to walk that twenty-three-mile March of Dimes Walk America again. I was not in the same shape; it had been a tough year. But my friends encouraged me and I also had a birthday cake waiting at the end. My hands and feet swelled, the blisters on my feet hurt, and I ended up walking in my socks for the last mile. I wanted to give up, but at every checkpoint, my friends from the four-wheel-drive club cheered me on. I did it! The pledge money was more than $125 this time.

I hope to find the tools to carry on.

CHAPTER 12

HOPE IN NEW CHAPTERS

AT A FALL race at the Bodacious track in Columbia, Virginia, I helped out with the money at the gate. Jamie and I stayed with my friend Dave and his family, who understood how nervous I was because Eric would be there. The camping area was large, and I kept myself busy; I didn't have time to think about where somebody else was. The gate was far away from the motor cross and drag strip. My friend Betty always watched my back, so to speak. She had been my cheerleader through the divorce.

Although I was staying with Dave, a single guy kept flirting with me. Tom invited Jamie and me to swim in the James River to cool off. Tom had an outgoing personality and was a lot of fun, something I hadn't had in a long time. He asked if he could take us home after the two-day event. About a month later, he invited me to his sister's wedding. "I can't wait to show you off," he said. I felt like I was walking on a cloud.

A month before deer season, he left a half-gallon of liquid on my coffee table. When hunting season began, he came by to pick it up. "Oops, I threw it out," I told him. "It lost its carbonation." At first he shook his head, but then he laughed.

I couldn't pay for the therapist anymore, because Eric dropped me from his insurance, and my insurance had not started yet. I had to go to a new facility, and they took me off the medication I had been on and put me on something else. I felt so good that I took myself off all the medications. I stopped therapy. I was tired of being teased for walking around like a zombie.

I was having fun with Tom; I went to my first Halloween party as an adult. We went on some camping trips up in the mountains and met these brothers Tom knew. They allowed us to camp on their property. The wallpaper in their house was Sears catalogue pages. The refrigerator was the creek that ran away from the house. At night, we cuddled around the campfire and talked.

It was not all a bed of roses; at times I couldn't concentrate and would cry at my situation. What would I do about the house? Eric wanted to sell it. Where would I live?

Work and school were going well, except for one practical joker who sent me to look for half-tone dots and a paper stretcher. I fell for his antics many times, and everyone laughed, especially the men. I laughed too, but only to fit in. At that time, the printing industry was 80 percent men.

I graduated from Richmond Technical School and finally had the initiative to look for an apartment. It had to be in the district were Jamie could continue going to the same school; she'd had enough upheaval in her life. Rent for a year was crazy. I had no credit in my name; therefore, every apartment complex wanted the first year's rent in advance. So when the house sold, I paid a full year's rent at an apartment within walking distance for the school.

Tom had every quality I looked for in a man; he coached little league and basketball, enjoyed older people, and liked to have fun. We did some four-wheel-drive racing and did almost everything together. He was the life of the party and had a lot of friends. He treated me like a princess. He and Jamie got along. Tom lived with his parents, who had a swimming pool. He appeared to work hard as a mechanic at his family business. I overlooked his drinking as he didn't drink all the time.

In the fall, Tom asked me to marry him on the steps of the

apartment. He gave me a half-karat diamond in orange-blossom setting. The diamond was set in black background. I couldn't believe it. I was taking a printing class at Henrico Trade School. Most of my classmates made letterhead, but I made my wedding announcements and thank-you cards.

Tom asked my daddy if he would give us his blessing. They had a few drinks after that; then we asked my parents to help us plan the wedding. My mother and I went to Peckville to meet with my grandmother. Grandma and I looked at patterns; she measured me; and I picked out the material. She made the most beautiful dress using the five patterns I liked and mailed it to me. The dress was a perfect fit.

We went to visit Father Stockert at Our Lady of Lourdes. We talked to him about getting married in the Catholic Church. I filled out the forms to have my marriage to Eric annulled; since we had not gotten married in the church, the process went quickly. Mama and Daddy really liked Tom.

In December, a story I wrote about Christmas in a Jeep was published in *Off the Road East Magazine*. In the spring, I participated in the March of Dimes Walk America again, but this time I prepared better. I walked about two miles a day beforehand to get ready. I took of my rings off and kept my hands up to keep the circulation going. I purchased better walking shoes. My time was better, and I felt better after the walk. My pledge money went up, and I was happy and not quite so sore.

Tom came over drunk and broke; he seemed to be that way more often as we got closer to the wedding. I began to have misgivings about getting married. We rode around for hours and talked about our future together. I told him about my previous experience; he said he would not let that happen again, and I believed him.

Me and Jamie at Tom and my wedding.

Tom and I planned the wedding; we talked about who would do what and who would be involved. Some of our friends made mints and all the bouquets. We planned a large Catholic Polish wedding. We had six bridesmaids, including Jamie, and Janice was the maid of honor. We had six groomsmen, a flower girl, and a ring bearer. My roommate from my institutional days was the musician; she played the violin.

We picked the music together, except for one song from *The Sound of Music*, "Climb Every Mountain." I was on top of the world. We rode to the reception in his grandmother's Cadillac; we'd wanted to ride in the Jeep, but Tom's family changed our minds. The reception was held at Confederate Hills Country Club. A lot of my friends helped my mom and me decorate; it took weeks to make the favors.

My mother cooked all the food, and her friends helped serve it. It was mostly Polish food—stuffed cabbage, poppy-seed rolls—my mother cooked for weeks and froze what could be frozen. She made homemade cherry tarts and cannoli. A friend of hers made the cake. Members of the Polish American Club danced in full ethnic costume. The band played Polish American music; there were thirteen cases of liquor and I couldn't count how many kegs of beer. Several of Daddy's friends served as bartenders.

We had all the trimmings I did not have when I eloped with Eric: throwing the bouquet to the single women; throwing the garter to the single men. There was a Polish tradition: The maid of honor put on an apron. Then she put an apron on me and a scarf, known as a babushka, on my head. Guests then put money in our aprons and they circled around me, while Tom tried to pull me away. He tried many times before he got me out of that circle. After drinking a lot of alcohol, some of the groomsmen pushed guests into the swimming pool, tuxedos, gowns, and all. Someone hid me in the bathroom, so I avoided the pool dunking.

We left very late that night. We'd planned to drive off in an open Jeep, but Tom switched to his uncle's new Thunderbird. Tom's friend from New Jersey stayed in the room next to our honeymoon suite, Tom stayed up and talked and partied with his friend, and I soaked my feet, which were swollen from dancing so much.

In the morning, we left for Niagara Falls, stopping in Pittsburg the first night. Tom did not feel very well, so I drove most of the way to Pittsburgh. At the hotel, he picked me up off my feet and carried me across the threshold. When we arrived at the hotel on the New York side of the falls, I heard someone calling my name as we walked across the parking lot. I looked up and there, five stories up, was one of my coworkers, yelling, "Have a good honeymoon! Pretend I'm not here!"

Tom was romantic. We took a cruise on the *Maid of the Mist*, which took us behind the falls. Even wearing our rain gear, it was fun and romantic. We drove to the Canadian side of the falls and sat and listened and watched the fast-moving water with mystery and wonder.

We returned home. Jamie met us, as she'd stayed in the apartment while we were away. We both returned to work, although it was not long after the wedding. I was asked to take charge of the second shift (3:00 p.m. to 11:00 p.m.) in the reprint department. Tom and I discussed the promotion, which came with a raise, and agreed that financially it would help, particularly since we were looking for a house.

In the fall, we found a house in Charles City County about thirty-five minutes from our workplaces. Jamie stayed with a friend so she could complete her senior year at Henrico High School. She came home on weekends, and Tom bought her a car. She was gone most of the time, as she worked part-time at a restaurant in Richmond. Tom bought an early Christmas present for me—a yellow Labrador retriever that I named CC. I soon fell in love with CC; he learned quickly to obey commands.

I applied for a job as account manager and got it. I was working hard on a career that had never been my dream, but I was good at it. I handled more than sixteen national magazines.

Perhaps because I could not get pregnant, my sex drive was completely out of control. I was high on love for Tom and wanted to give him the world, yet I couldn't give him a baby. My desire to please him included role-playing activities, such as putting on a raincoat, ringing the front doorbell, and when he came to the door, well, the raincoat went away, and it was a treat, not a trick. During holidays, somehow there were more promiscuous activities than I could think up in my head.

Tom was an outdoorsman. He loved hunting, fishing, water-skiing, snow skiing, and going out with the guys. As the years went on, it seemed that more of the outdoor activities were "out with the guys" nights, including going to cockfights.

It was during this time that I burst into the company president's office, insisting—in explicit language—that I was going to take his job. In due time, a magistrate signed a green warrant to admit me to Saint Mary's Hospital. I learned I had a mental illness called manic depression, which would be with me the rest of my life. It was controllable, but not curable. Anxiety mounted each day I was in the hospital, away from my husband, my family, and my work. I was not sure if I would be able to return to work. There were so many uncertainties rambling through my head, thoughts racing one after another, and I had no control of them.

The medication had a lot of side effects; one of them made me feel stiff, as if my body were moving in slow motion. I cried at the thought of having to go back to work, filled with shame and guilt over what I'd done that day in August 1981. One medication required me to have blood drawn every other day. I felt like a pin cushion; the places where they drew blood turned into ugly black-and-blue marks. I wore long sleeve shirts to cover the marks. Strange people entered my room announcing their titles—occupational, physical, art, and music therapists. I recognized their faces, but in the cloud of the medication, I couldn't remember their names.

I felt like I was being watched every moment. Walking and moving were an effort. Evening therapy was meant to build skills, but I didn't see how it helped. In fact, some of the relaxation exercises made me more restless and anxious; I often waited for the relaxation tape to end. I felt I had no control of what I could or could not do. I felt hopeless.

The only private place was in the bathroom, and I wasn't convinced that was really private. When I wanted to shave my legs, a nurse had to bring the razor, stay in the bathroom while I shaved, and then take the razor back.

Visitors only came at certain times. I was fortunate my parents, siblings, husband, and stepdaughter (love daughter), and a few friends came to visit. One day the wife of the vice president of the company I worked for came to visit. Janet talked about God, Jesus, and her prayers for me. I thought that if someone were praying for me, it meant I was dying. But as she talked about trusting God, her calming voice and gentle actions appealed to me more than the relaxation tapes.

Where was hope?

My husband was frustrated, blaming me for the situation we were in now. Our life now had boundaries—no alcohol, taking medication on time, seeing a psychiatrist monthly—that were completely different than he had expected. His once-vibrant wife was now lifeless as a dish rag.

Janet invited me to her home after I left the hospital. She served me on china, and we ate in a formal dining room. She treated me with love and respect; we prayed before the meal. To me it was fancy: chicken salad in little pastry cups and fruit in china cups. Janet gave me a Bible, only four inches by five inches in size; it became a part of me. I carried in my pocketbook and kept it near the bed. This little Bible contained the New Testament. She inscribed it, "Presented for Mary from the Lord, September 17, 1981."

"My soul, waits in silence for God only, for my hope is from him" (Psalm 62:5).

Tom just could not support a wife with a mental illness. It was difficult and lonely as he spent more time away. It was several months before I became aware that he was "hunting" two-legged deer. In February 1982, he left.

I felt hopeless.

CHAPTER 13
HOPE IN FILLING THE EMPTINESS

I WAS DEVASTATED. My friend Janice took me to my psychiatrist, and we worked on coping skills to help me stay out of the hospital. She truly was an angel, making sure I was safe and had my medication, and staying with me for support.

A friend from work and her husband moved into my house. Living with strangers is not easy; at times I felt it was not my house, as though the common areas belonged to someone else, who watched TV programs I did not like. My dog and their dog got along, sometimes, but the extra money came in handy.

My supervisor sat down and told me I was making errors, and I had a choice: I could either go to the employee assistant program (EAP) or no longer be an account manager. Well, since I had house payments, car payments, household bills, and a lawyer's bill, I went to EAP. I met with Harriet, a licensed clinical social worker. At first, it was rough; I didn't want to be there, but I had to meet with her to keep my job. Then I was looking through a magazine called *NSR* (published by the National Shorthand Reporters Association), an account I managed, I came across an article about recovering from manic depression. I was so excited that I called the author of the article that night. We met in

Washington, DC, where she was visiting a relative. We developed a strategy to start a manic depression group in Richmond.

Through much communication and the help of MCV and Richmond Behavioral Health, we started the group. It was difficult, at times, to stay focused between the manic highs and the downward slopes. Even though I tried hard to stay focused, I was removed from my account manager's job and asked to work the 3:00 p.m. to 11:00 p.m. shift in prepress. I went from a business suit, heels, and a briefcase to a T-shirt and jeans. I was still going through the grief process over the loss of my perks, when the supervisor came and said, "Your old customer is coming through this afternoon. You can take the afternoon off if you want." He was trying to protect me from shame, but I was determined to hold onto my pride and stay at my desk. The customer came through, and I was polite, but the tears flowed after he left.

When I moved to the second shift, the manic depressive group disbanded after a few months. I had a bell collection and belonged to a bell collectors group. One night the bells started talking to me. I was alone in the house and decided to call my brother and his wife. My parents came and persuaded me to let them take me to the hospital. When I was discharged, I stayed at their house at night and went home to feed my animals during the day. I now had three dogs. A coworker came to the house and prayed over me in an evangelical manner. My dad asked her to leave.

I listened to the radio. I called into the station often and got to know the DJs. I invited one DJ to come to my house for dinner, and he came! In my fantasy world, he became my newfound boyfriend, until I started stalking him. I would be on his doorstep when he got off work; I followed him home several times. Finally he had enough, and he said, "Next time you follow me, I will call the police." I never followed him again.

I found a new place to fill the void in my life. The Virginia National Guard hung out at the Holiday Inn Bar on Wednesdays, Fridays, and Saturdays twice a month. One Friday night, I was attracted to a helicopter pilot named Wayne. We danced, and I drank a bottle of beer. I dreamed about him. He invited me to his house, and I went. The only thing was the house had nothing in it but his dog and bedroom furniture, as his wife had just left him and taken most of the furniture. It didn't matter, he asked me out again, and I liked being liked. I only saw him when he came to Richmond, but that was good enough for me. He said he would move to Richmond.

A friend of mine needed a place to stay; she wanted to move in with me, and so I said yes. She worked a different shift, and that seemed to go well, until I felt like I was having a baby. When I told her that the baby was Wayne's and that she was having Wayne's baby too, she called my parents. They came right away, and I told them I was having Wayne's baby and I was in labor. When we got to the hospital, I was admitted to the ICU. I was disoriented for several days. I had stopped taking my medication. While I was in the ICU, I hit a male nurse and knocked him off his chair. "That one's for Wayne."

My girlfriend called Wayne's commanding officer and said Wayne had to see me as I was having his baby. After a week or so, he came; he already knew I couldn't have children. During the 1980s, a patient could leave the floor escorted by a guest. He and I left not only the floor, we left the hospital; he took me for ice cream about four miles down the road. I never said a word. I wanted to go home. I called him on the phone him excessively, and left voice mail after voice mail.

There came a time when I was no longer interested in going to bars with my friends. I got disappointed when men didn't want to dance with me because I led when dancing. I volunteered at Children's Hospital instead; that lasted about a year. I loved making the children laugh with charades, reading to them, and pulling them around in a wagon. I met a young girl from Beirut. Her arm and part of her face had been blown up during a bomb attack. We became friends, and I gave her a Bible. A couple of months later, she witnessed me having a manic episode. She asked my parents if she could visit me.

I had no boundaries and little fear of consequences; often I put myself in harm's way. Driving down the interstate, I saw a couple sitting in lawn chairs next to their car; a little further down the road I saw another couple walking. I asked the couple walking if they wanted a ride, as the nearest service station was miles away. They climbed into my very small car, and I took them to the nearest service station. I left them there, and a tow truck followed me to the car on the interstate, where he picked up the car, and I picked up the other couple. One couple was from Canada, and the other from France. The car was left at the service station. While they waited for their car to be fixed, all five of us squeezed into my small car, and we went out to supper at a quaint mom-and-pop restaurant in Highland Springs. When I took them back to their car, it was way past their reservation time at a camp ground in Williamsburg. I invited them to spend the night in my backyard. They put up their tents, popped a bottle of good wine, and we spent an evening exchanging cultures. They called me their angel of the highway. At Christmas, I received cards from those people of the highway.

That year, we had an ice and snow storm. Just before my house was a curve on the road. Around 9:00 p.m., I heard a loud crash. I put my coat on and went outside to find a car in the ditch. In the car were to oversized women, who were very drunk. It took a while to get them out of the car and across the road to my house. I made coffee to sober then up. Next morning the police came to the door asking if I had seen the people who had been in the car in the ditch. The women told the police that I'd saved their lives, as they would have frozen to death. Their family members had been looking for them all night. I never learned their names.

In the spring, I picked up a young man walking in the middle of the country road. When he got in the car, I sensed that he was strung out on drugs. "How far are you going?" I asked.

"Just up the street," he answered.

"Where are you going?" he asked.

I said, "To church."

He said, "Let me out of here. Church is not for me." I never saw him again.

I took home strangers I met in bars, desperately hoping to fill an empty place in my heart. It didn't matter who as long as they just gave me some attention.

When I told these stories to my parents or friends, their response was, "Are you crazy? They could have taken everything you had!" I'd tell my therapist, and we'd talk about the emptiness. But what can fill an endless emptiness?

I hope to find what will fill the void.

CHAPTER 14
HOPE IN LIGHT

I HEARD THAT my psychiatrist was giving a talk about manic depression. He said if I could find a ride, he would give me a pass for the night. I found a ride and heard him speak. Afterward, I talked to him about the group that I'd tried to start. He asked me to come to his office. I brought a shopping bag full of information and let him keep it. We talked about starting a new group; this was in 1985.

I spoke to my shift supervisor about this idea, because it meant I would have to leave work early three hours every month. He agreed. The group became known as the Manic Depressive Support Group. We had speakers and mini workshops, and I became the president. My doctor came to every meeting and arranged for a psychiatric nurse to be present. The more speakers we had, the more I learned about my own illness and the more I was able control the impulses.

Therapy was going well now, but the first year was difficult, she was Jewish and I was Catholic, it took a while for us to get in sync. I wrote in a journal, and she read it. I rarely wrote about me, but more about my friends and the men in my life. She said I got lost in their lives; it was my life she wanted to read about.

Finally I wrote about the secret I'd kept since I was twelve years old. I showed the journal entry to my therapist—the rape, who was involved, why I kept it a secret all these years, that I'd never even told my parents. With the help of this therapist, I told my parents at last, and I was set free.

I wanted to start over, to set out on my own. I wanted to seek my own religion. I started going to a new church, bursting through the doors of a small ecumenical church in eastern Henrico. "I want God's help," I said. I wanted to be somewhere where people accepted me, and this was it. The members of this little church took time to get to know me. When I was in the hospital, they came to see me behind locked doors. They let me teach, preach, and learn the Bible.

One day my godmother needed a ride back to Pennsylvania, and I went to Mass with her at Sacred Heart Catholic Church. After Mass, I took her back to her house on the mountain and went back down to the church and watched the priest baptize seven babies. I felt like Zaccheus in a tree, waiting to see Jesus. I met with the young priest and had a two-and-a-half-hour confession. We talked about my illness, my membership at the other church, and everything else in-between. His last words to me were, "Go back to Virginia to love and serve the Lord."

I had a six-and-half-hour trip back to Virginia to think about his words. It was not a coincidence that Father Stockert was serving as sacramental priest in a Catholic mission that met in a barber shop in New Kent, Virginia. I missed receiving the Eucharist and going to Mass each day. I started teaching kindergarten and first-grade Sunday school. At the groundbreaking for Saint Elizabeth Ann Seton, I was asked to serve as Eucharistic minister and minister to the sick.

This was the first transition in my life, the first time I chose lightness instead of darkness. I was moving toward God's light.

My hope is in him.

CHAPTER 15
HOPE IN DREAMS

I HAD A dream, through seventeen years and two ex-husbands, to build a log home on a lake. I kept a small picture on my refrigerator door all that time. I owned the house in Charles City and that is about all I owned; even the car I drove belonged to the bank.

I met an old friend from high school at a church Christmas party. Fred was a realtor and asked what would make me sell my little Ponderosa in Charles City. I told him about my dream to build a log home. I thought he was making small talk at the party, but to my surprise in January he called me about selling my house. Fred showed me a lot in New Kent on Kent Lake. I knew it was the place for my log home, but we encountered hurdle after hurdle.

First I had to find someone to build it. One was being built not far from my lot; that is where I met Mac, who specialized in log-home construction. We made a connection right off the bat. He told me to look into a company in Tennessee. I went to Tennessee to meet the sales person, who agreed to review the plans I already had. He showed me the cartograph that brought up the cost and building instructions. I took it to back to Mac. Next, I needed financing.

I went to ten different banks to get a construction loan; one loaned me the money, with the following condition: every Friday the loan officer could come down and take pictures of the log home's progress.

I was my own general contractor on this huge project and didn't know a darn thing about building a house. The sales person gave me a checklist. The printing company was printing a magazine called *Log Home Living*. One issue had a checklist of things you needed to build a log home. It included grading the land, selecting a location for the foundation; storing the logs on your property; getting electrical, plumbing, and building permits; checking with the local building inspector; and last but not least where to rent a port-a-potty.

I had a buyer for my house in Charles City, but the person backed out of the deal. I was upset, until my supervisor said his son and daughter-in-law were looking for a first home. They looked at the house and purchased it. As the log home was being built, I thanked every person who worked on it, but most of all I thanked God for sending me the crew.

My dream home, 1989.

The house sits sideways on the property, in keeping with county codes, fifteen feet on both sides from house to property line. Some thought I would get depressed because of the bills; others thought I would be manic because of the stress. The men at the printing company took bets on whether I would be in a psychiatric hospital before the house was completed. None of that happened.

Frank was still on the edges of my life, I guess I meant more to him than he did to me, because after the house was complete and I had been living there for several months, Frank had a desire to get married. However, I didn't. Getting an engagement ring confused me. I went into the hospital, as that was a safe place to break up with him. I felt really bad. We were at a crossroads in our lives; I was moving on, and he was not. This too was new for me, being the one to change direction.

The printing company asked me to be on its diversity team, which was part of an effort to break down barriers in the printing world among African American, Caucasian, ethnic groups of all kinds, gay people, and the mentally ill. Serving on this team was a real eye opener. I had been naïve about how people were treated, until I became one of those people.

My dad and I were in a Christmas parade; in front of us were a lot of people in yellow. After the parade, I asked what all the yellow was about and learned it is the international color of hope. I started wearing more yellow. Hope became a motto to live by. It stood for:

HELPING MYSELF FIRST, then others;

OVERCOMING MY OWN barriers;

PREVENTING MENTAL PAIN through prayer, prescriptions, psychiatrist and prayer;

EDUCATING MYSELF AND others.

This encouraged me to continue my journey of hope.

I prepared a talk on the rights and responsibilities for the mentally ill, which I hoped to present to the Virginia General Assembly. This was the first time I was moved to speak for those who could not speak for themselves. I included insurance issues, since one year I used all my mental-health insurance and did not have coverage for two months. I spoke about holding on to one's dignity during a crisis situation. Many of the medications prescribed for mental issues cause dental and eye issues, and no insurance, Medicaid does not included, provides adequate dental and eye care. Housing is another great challenge, as many people with mental illness end up homeless or without adequate housing. Since that first time, I have addressed the Virginia General Assembly many times. Sometimes the presentations were not heard by the entire assembly; only a small group heard the people who required so much courage to present.

Sometimes the smallest sound can make the loudest noise. Hope is not about being heard, but about finding the courage to speak out.

I hope the politicians can hear our hope.

CHAPTER 16

HOPE IN A RELATIONSHIP WITH GOD

IN APRIL 1990, my supervisor at the printing company asked me to go on a spiritual weekend. He said, "I will okay your vacation time, so if you say yes, I'll get my wife to pick you up on Thursday, and you will come back on Sunday."

The weekend was a birthday gift to myself. I met his wife at their home. She took me and another person to a place on a dirt road in Montpelier, Virginia, called Shalom House, a Catholic retreat in the middle of nowhere. The closest paved street was more than a mile away. It had a pond, ducks, and more than twenty people I'd never seen before. My supervisor told me only to have a good time and take it all in. That's exactly what I did.

I was not able to sit still for long periods. While the others were sitting quietly in the chapel, I weeded all the flower beds. I was quiet; I was just moving and being quiet. I talked to the flowers and asked them what stage of growth they were in. Sounds weird, doesn't it? The good thing was, they didn't answer me back.

The days passed quickly as there was a lot to do and observe. On Sunday morning, around daybreak, I had to go to the bathroom. Six other women were staying in my room; lucky for me, the bathroom was near my bed. I sat on the toilet and watched a cloud come up from the nearby pond. I watched it come through the window and into the bathroom and surround me. I yelled at it in my head, "Go away. I don't want to be sick. Just go away."

I knew what a manic episode felt like and I didn't want one then or any other time. So naturally I fought the cloud surrounding me. As the cloud pulled me tight, I heard a voice say, "Be calm and be still." But I continued to fight and tell it to go away. The more I struggled, the tighter the cloud surrounded me. Finally I said, "Okay, okay, okay. I'll be calm and still." I said it over and over until the cloud went back to the pond. I sat there, wondering what to do next. It was a long time before I left the bathroom.

By God's divine intervention, one of my roommates was a medical doctor. I told her what happened, and after thinking for a moment, she said in a stern voice, "If the voice says be calm and be still, then shut up and listen."

As everyone was waking up, I went to the spiritual director's room. A woman came to the door and said to me, "Don't ruin it for everyone else." That was one answer I didn't expect. I asked again to speak to the spiritual director. A man came to the door and asked how he could help me. When I told him what had happened, he asked me to walk with him. We walked back and forth from the retreat house to the dirt road several times. I told him what had happened just several hours before. I repeated the events till I could talk no more. He just listened, which was good for me.

The rest of the day went as scheduled, until the ending, which they call a closing. At the closing, each person attending for the first time was asked to get up and say what he or she had gotten out of the weekend. When I approached the podium, I noticed an older woman leaning against the wall. I had not noticed her before, but she looked oddly familiar. As I spoke about experiencing closeness to the Lord, the old woman smiled and nodded in approval. When I finished my remarks, the old woman smiled again, waved, turned, and vanished into the wall. That was the last time I saw my imaginary friend Judy; I realized later that she knew I would no longer need her, now that I had faith to get me through.

On Sunday afternoon, my supervisor and his wife took me to my car. I went to my log home and slept in my own bed that night. I slept like I had never slept before.

The weekend's theme had been God's Chosen One. That included everyone, not just me. I was on fire for Jesus Christ. I even wrote him a letter in which I promised to work in his world and help those with mental illness. I promised I would keep my faith and trust in him.

On Monday morning, on my way to work, I went by my parents' house to let them know where I'd been and that I'd heard a voice telling me to be calm and be still, although at that time I was neither. I was so excited about the weekend. My parents thought I should see my psychiatrist, and without hesitation, I said, "Let's go."

We met my psychiatrist at the hospital. He and my parents thought I should be admitted. The psychiatric floor was full. We were diverted to another hospital in south Richmond. The doctor met us there; he asked me to comply with my parents' request and stay. I stayed for three days. I had fun. I played board games, read some, relaxed a lot, and told the patients and staff about my weekend.

The community of folks who ran the weekend didn't quite know how to handle my hospital stay after my Cursillo. That's what it was called, the Cursillo, the best-kept secret of the Catholic Church. People I met during the weekend visited me. Some wrote me cards. I had never been so enveloped in love during a hospital stay.

Cursillo is a short study of Christianity that started in Majorca, Spain, in 1940. A group of men wanted to attract young single men to the church. They developed a program, inspired by the Holy Spirit, to bring the light of Christ into people's daily lives and help them bear God's fruit. It was intended to be a symbolic journey of meditation and self-reflection. It became a spirit of brotherhood among fellow pilgrims striving to achieve a life fully given to the love of God and man. It eventually grew to include married men and women as well. There was an interruption during World War II, but the movement picked back up in 1948. Not all bishops were in favor of the Cursillo mission; in 1954 the new bishop in Majorca put an end to the weekends there. This was not much of a setback, since the Cursillo had already spread to South and Central America, Canada, Mexico, Portugal, Puerto Rico, Great Britain, Ireland, France, Germany, Austria, Italy, Yugoslavia, Japan, Korea, Taiwan, the Philippines, Sri Lanka, and several African countries.

The first Cursillo in the United States was held in Waco, Texas, in 1957. The key figures were three men from Spain, Father Gabriel Fernandez and two airmen, Bernardo Vidal and Augustine Palomino, who were training with the US Air Force. By 1959, eighteen weekends had been held in Waco. The movement spread to Phoenix, Arizona, throughout the southwest, and by 1960, it was in New York. In mid-1960, the movement began in the Episcopal Church. Until 1961, the weekends were held in Spanish.

Other denominations adopted the Cursillo movement, calling it the Emmaus Walk. The first English weekend was held in San Angelo, Texas. In 1966, Pope Paul VI addressed the movement at its first worldwide reunion, and in 1980 Pope John Paul II addressed the movement as well. By 1981, 160 dioceses in the United States had been introduced to the Cursillo movement. The first Cursillo in the Richmond diocese was in 1964, and since then the city has had 451 weekends, with men and women. So this was no small Christian movement, I'd found myself in.

I went back to work, 2:00 in the afternoon to 10:00 at night. My doctor suggested that I get home by 11:00 p.m. to get a good night's sleep. The evening shift suited my lifestyle. I asked my supervisor if I could start a support group called Stress at the Press. We met for several months and discussed topics like grief, working mothers, and causes of stress.

I was volunteering with the Manic Depressive Support Group, Stress at the Press, and teaching Sunday School. And I had just completed my dream house.

Jesus provides hope when we are broken and healing when we are hurting. Hope is my journey, but not my destination, because with each grace, we are directed toward a new destination.

CHAPTER 17
HOPE IN SPIRITUAL DIRECTION

I KNOCKED ON the door and asked to speak to Sister Lucy, a Comboni Missionary nun I'd met in the 1960s. Sister Lucy had been to Africa and was now at a convent in Richmond. She became my spiritual director. I met with her ever two weeks. We spent hours together, discussing my work, home life, church life, mental illness, and anything in-between.

When I told her about my new relationship with a man I'd known for many years, a coworker, she asked about his spiritual life, about which I knew nothing. I told her his name was Sam, and he was willing to go to church with me and someday become Catholic.

Sam lived in Charlotte, North Carolina, but visited me every weekend. After four months of traveling back and forth, he got a job at the printing company where I worked. He had worked there too, before moving back to Charlotte to be with his son and parents.

I started the annulment process and, through that process, he had to see my therapist for six sessions. We went to pre-marriage class, which was required by the church, and he went to Mass with me. I seemed to be doing the right things, but I was ignoring the red flags: he came to Virginia with a punch bowl full of quarters, drank on a daily basis, drove without a driver's license, and did not pay his taxes for several years.

We got married at Saint Elizabeth Ann Seton Catholic Church. It was a small wedding, followed by a reception at the log home. Sam promised me the world. "I'll go to church with you, become a Catholic, and stop drinking." I believed him on all counts. We went to the Bahamas for a honeymoon and he got really drunk on the *Bahama Mama* boat trip. I invited Sister Lucy to the house for vespers shortly after we got married, and it was a unique experience for both of us. I was in my glory, but I'm not sure how he felt.

I met with the chaplain at Saint Mary's Hospital. I told him that I had not received any prayer or religious time while I was a patient on the behavioral health floor. He gave me a challenge: what would I offer on the floor? I told him I'd have to pray about how to lead a prayer service. We met a week later. I told him my ideas, and he asked, "Did you pray about it?" I answered that I had. He got permission for me to volunteer every other Sunday, and another ministry started. I took my red bag that said "It's a jingle out there." Inside was a cassette player, a flag with an emblem indicating the liturgical season, two electric candles, a couple of Bibles, and the agenda for the week, which included a reading from the book of Psalms, the gospel reading of the day, and a reflection. Then we'd say the Lord's Prayer and a benediction together. All the readings were read by the patients. Sometimes there was music, played or sung by a patient. They called me Church Lady, a nickname I bear proudly, regarding it as noble and magnificent as any ambassadorial title. I truly felt like an ambassador for Christ each time I met with the patients who were where I once was. I did this for six or seven years.

During this period, the priest at Saint Mary's suggested I go to the Virginia Institute of Pastoral Care, known as VIPCARE. There were six other students in my class, most had undergraduate degrees. All of us were seeking pastoral studies. I spoke freely about the journey on which God had set me. My professor commissioned me to go forth and work with people who had mental illness in the community. She laid hands on my head in front of the other students, something I had never experienced. But I accepted it and trusted in God's vocational power.

While others gave long dissertations about their particular subjects, I made a mini-calendar, the size of a business card. Working at the printing company gave me some idea about how to do it—to type, print, cut out, collate, and glue the spine. I had the idea long before I knew what I would do with it. I called the calendar *Hope, There Is Hope*, and for each quarter added quotations related to helping, overcoming, preventing, and educating. Some quotations were from scripture; some were from friends and family. I gave a talk about the word hope and what it meant to me. Then I gave each student a copy.

After the two-year program in parish pastoral care I received a certificate from VIPCARE . I didn't know where I was going, though I knew immediately that I'd gone the wrong way when I approached the dean at Virginia Union Theological Seminary. I asked him when I could start. He asked what my undergraduate degree was in. I looked at him like he was nuts. He said, "You have to have an undergraduate degree to go to this school." I looked him in the eye and said, "Jesus didn't have a cell phone, a briefcase, or a degree," and walked out.

When I got in the car, I cried. Had I slipped into a manic state? What was I doing? What was I thinking? Why did I say something like that to the dean? It was a case of my mouth opening before I thought about what I was saying. That was a symptom of mania.

God, you led me to this point. Now where was I to go? The words came back to me: be calm and be still. So I sat in the car—no radio, no music—just silence for more than hour. Then I went to work; it was nearly 2:00 p.m.

I passed the baton to next president of the Manic Depressive Support group. I had been president for five years. I learned from my first experience at starting a group not to do it all by myself. The next person was ready to take over. It was time.

I put my energy into the search for a curriculum that met my needs. The priest at Saint Mary's Hospital suggested LIMEX, the Loyola Institute for Ministry Extension Program, supported by the Richmond diocese. I knew I didn't have the writing skills to undertake a four-year program. With a little prompting from the priest, I talked to the program director.

I had to write a biography and have two people endorse me to get into the program. I had a new job at the printing company, as a purchase agent for pre-press supplies. My hours were 8:30 a.m. to 4:30 p.m., It was not by chance that the person who sat next to me in the office was an assistant professor at a local university. He read my biography and gave it back to me. It looked like graffiti with red marks, but he was my saving grace. Line by line, he edited my first attempt at writing at a university level.

Requirements were placed before me like roadblocks; with every one, I rose to the challenge. I trusted God, through prayer, to help me through the next four years. Twelve very different people came together in that first class, meeting in a church in the west end of Richmond. Our facilitator was a nun I already knew. That first year, we seemed to be in a boat, all of us rowing in different directions. Two people dropped out after the syllabus was presented. There was so much reading and so much writing. I would wake up at 5:00 a.m. and do much of my reading. It was a three-hour class and for every hour of classroom work, there was one hour of homework.

Sam asked me to quit school several times. His son, Jeff, came from North Carolina to live with us. Jeff was in the ninth grade and had just been implanted with a new pacemaker. I was more frightened by the pacemaker than about him living with us. Again, I relied on the advice of Sister Lucy. "Stay steadfast in your trust in God," she would tell me. I continued school.

The first year Jeff lived with us required quite an adjustment. He relied on me for the emotional support that his father could not supply. One day, Jeff asked me if alcoholism was genetic; if it was, he didn't want to catch it. Jeff and I had many discussions about alcoholism.

The Loyola group of ten moved to a house on church property in Saint John's, my old parish. One member passed away and another dropped out, but we continued to meet. We made up our own schedule, which was fine as long as we met the requirements. We took the summers off to regroup. When we came back, our facilitator was asked to move to Long Island, to her main convent. We chose someone from the group to facilitate and continued to study.

Grace, set me free to let God work within me.

CHAPTER 18
GRACE FOR THE JOURNEY

TWICE A MONTH, I ventured to Saint Mary's from New Kent, a mere thirty-five minutes away. I would go to the chapel to pray before going to the behavioral health floor and doing the prayer service on Sunday mornings. I also took communion to the Catholics on the floor, and after the service, I met with those who wanted to talk. The prayer service became the theme throughout my years in the Loyola program. It satisfied my craving to give back to the community.

I sent the agenda and reflection via e-mail to my fellow students, friends, and several priests, to confirm I was on the right track. I asked for comments, and took them as constructive feedback and made adjustments accordingly. I began to be asked to speak at workshops more frequently.

While visiting the Comboni Missionary sisters, I asked for prayer for Jeff's health; he needed a new pace maker. Overhearing the conversation, Father Conroy said he would come to the house to anoint Jeff and give him the sacrament of the anointing of the sick. Jeff had been baptized Catholic when he was almost six. Now this was quite an event for Sam and Jeff. A priest is coming to the house to do what? Finally, both of them agreed, and Father showed up at the house, after getting a little lost since we lived in the country.

I took off work and stayed with Jeff in the hospital. Father had said he would meet us there, but he didn't show, which was very unusual. It turned out he'd had a heart attack at the rectory earlier that day. Several days later. I took four nuns to the funeral mass at Sacred Heart Cathedral. His last act was one of kindness to Jeff.

The local ceremony for our graduation from the Loyola program was held at Saint John's Catholic Church. Present was a Presbyterian minister, my priest from Saint Elizabeth Ann Seton, the priest from Saint John's, and Bishop Walter Sullivan. My mother handled the catering, as only she could. Homemade cherry tarts, cream puffs, and an array of meat and bread trays. There was a punch bowl and glass cups. My mom knew how to put on a party in short order.

My in-laws came from North Carolina; most of my family came. Each person had his or her family at the graduation.

Toward the end of the ceremony I was awarded the Bishop Sullivan Jubilee 2000 Award for Recognition of Lay Discipleship. My father also received the same award. We were the only father and daughter from two different churches to be honored for the same award.

The formal graduation ceremony was on Sunday, May 14, 2000, on the campus of Loyola University in New Orleans. Two hundred and fifty graduates representing twenty-two different Catholic dioceses were present. We'd all gone through the same program, just in different localities. I was part of the ceremony, but I couldn't tell you how that came to be.

I brought a jar of water from New Kent and poured it into a large container. Water from all across the country was mixed together. I really enjoyed the symbolism. The waters were stirred together and used to bless the people present. Some received a master's in pastoral education; others received a master's in religious education. I received a certificate in pastoral care. Whether certificate or master's, we all did the same work over four years of study.

Off to the celebration! The commencement reception began to

the sounds of "When the Saints Go Marching In." The last verse stuck with me:

> O when the sun, begins to shine,
> O when the sun begins to shine,
> How I want to be in that number
> when the sun begins to shine.

We stayed for a week sightseeing. One day did not go well; Sam had too many bourbon and Cokes on Bourbon Street.

Dear Lord, give me the grace to have courage.

Chapter 19
GRACE TO SHARE SPIRITUALITY

I HAD BEEN at the printing company for almost twenty-five years and was ready to embark on a new vocation. I say vocation because at that time of my life I knew that God was with me, and the next part of my journey would include his presence. I had no idea where these four years of writing, studying, and sharing would take me.

First I thought about working in a hospital as a chaplain, but I found out I needed two more years of school, and the program was not friendly to my economic situation. Then I remembered Dr. Hamilton's commission to bring my gifts to wherever I was.

I started looking in other areas. I sent out more than fifty resumes, from Richmond to Newport News to Petersburg, all within a fifty-mile radius of my home. Sam showed me an ad in the newspaper for a supportive living counselor for Chesterfield County. I didn't have all the requirements, but I applied anyway. A letter came in the mail asking to come for an interview.

I had no experience driving around Chesterfield; it might well have been in another state. I got lost getting to the mental-health complex and had to apologize for my tardiness, not the best opening for an interview. I brought everything I needed for a good interview, including my transcripts, my thesis from Loyola, and a copy of the services I provided at Saint Mary's. I even copied the plaque that the Manic Depressive Support Group had given me when I retired from being president.

The doctor who interviewed me asked about my credentials and listened intently. I told him about my journey; I gave him my papers to keep. He ended by asking about the Catholic Church's annulment process. After I left his office, I looked up and said to God, "You sent me on a mission. I hope it is to get this job." I got no response; I waited (im)patiently. Three weeks later, I heard a song at Mass: "Here I am, Lord. Is it I, Lord?" And I left Mass crying. A friend came and counseled me. "What's wrong? One of your favorite sayings is, 'God qualifies the called.'"

The next morning the doctor called me and offered me the job. I quickly said yes, but I had to call him back, as I had planned a vacation that began the same day I was to begin my new vocation. My start date was moved back a week, and the two weeks' notice I gave the printing company included my vacation. It was awesome. The company gave me a going-away party: food, non-alcoholic sparkling grape drink, a photo album. Most of my coworkers wrote affirmations for me.

l I flew to Florida and spent time with my daughter and her children. Jamie had remarried, and I met my new granddaughter and spent time with the other two grandchildren, who had grown up way too quickly. The last morning I took time for myself in Epcot Center and Sea World, then flew home to Virginia. I needed that day to be just by myself, to find myself. I decided to stop using Mary and go back to the name I was born with, Maryalyce. All my legal documentation already had my legal name, so I just introduced myself as Maryalyce.

I started working as a supportive living counselor for Chesterfield County on August 21, 2000, not because I'd had a mental illness, but because God qualified me to do the job. I had been qualified through education from Loyola, but also through experience, from the school of hard knocks.

The vocation was not without challenge; I had to write a progress note for each client, each visit. At first writing them was difficult, because I realized that somewhere there were notes like them written about me. I tried hard not to be judgmental and just kept to the here and now and what I had seen with my own eyes.

Working in the field inspired me more than ever to speak for those who could not speak for themselves—regarding fair housing, equality, and insurance coverage for mental illness and dental and eye care. I had a bird's eye view, seeing the poverty people lived with just because they had a mental illness. We take so much for granted when it comes to human rights.

I worked because I liked working. When I graduated from Loyola, I was given a towel that said "Do What I Have Done." That is what I was doing, servicing those who were what I once was.

Once a year, Chesterfield County Mental Health had an employee appreciation week; on Wednesday, they had an employee dinner. In 2003, I was voted employee of the year by my peers. I was in a state of shock. I couldn't believe it. That night I called my parents. I was in tears, and when I mentioned that a doctor was at the dinner, my mother did not believe me; she thought I was getting sick. It saddens me that she focused on the pain of the 1980s and not on my recovery in the present moment.

I had been asked to be on a women's Cursillo weekend. During formation, a process in which team members get to know one another, my arm felt like something was moving up and down under the skin. I went to my doctor, and he sent me to a specialist. I tried physical therapy to no avail. The specialist did an MRI and a CAT scan. The pain kept me up nights, and I didn't like being on pain medication during working hours.

I had three crushed disks in my upper neck. It was up to me to decide the surgery time, but my doctor was leaving the practice, and the last surgery he'd perform was on the Thursday before the Cursillo weekend. I had a conversation with God. "Help yourself first before helping others." So I had the operation on Thursday, but a friend from Cursillo took me to the service on the last day of the retreat, much to Sam's and his mother's dismay. I was okay, in no pain and doing well, so I went and joined my team. The big collar I had to wear fit fine; it was not very fashionable, but it did the trick.

Several weeks later the perpetual calendar Sam had been working on was almost ready. My little business-card calendar was now a four-by five-inch book with colored butterflies. It was printed but needed to be spiral-bound. We took all the boxes to my parents' house as they had the most room. It took some time to collate all those little pieces of paper. Round and round the dining room table, putting this little calendar together.

My mother quality-controlled the project, and my father was just glad when it was over. The real *Hope, There Is HOPE* was born. I thanked everyone who had a part in putting the calendar together. The kid who couldn't spell cat using the letters C-A-T was now published.

Some vacations were good, and some were awful. Sam hid alcohol above the kitchen cabinets; at first, I didn't realize why he made so many trips to the kitchen. Then I stood outside the kitchen window and saw what he was doing. I spent our vacation at Nags Head outdoors reading a book, away from Sam. A hurricane came through, and we had to pack up and leave. Jeff had just arrived; there was no vacation for him.

There had been talk at work that a new department was being formed called the Intensive Community Treatment (ICT) team, which needed to have a peer specialist on board. The peer specialist had to have a mental illness. The director asked me. I was not sure at first as I was not fond of the title peer specialist. I felt like it put a stigma on top of a stigma. I told them if the title changed to recovery specialist, I would be on the team. My new supervisor followed my thought process and changed the title to clinician/recovery specialist.

We went to different community service boards to observe how they ran their ICT departments. I carried a full case load, just like any other clinician; I did not want to be treated any differently because of my mental illness. This team treated me as an equal.

One day, I found yellow post-it notes all around my commuter, urging me to apply for the Wellness Recovery Action Plan (WRAP) training organized by the Virginia Department of Mental Health and Substance Abuse. The first trainees were individuals from all over the state of Virginia. The program was designed by a woman from Vermont, Mary Ellen Copeland, and several of her colleagues who had been in the state hospital together.

Two facilitators from two different states came to train us. There were twelve in the class, and we met each day for one week at the Embassy Suites in Richmond. I wore yellow each day, and by the end of the week everyone knew that yellow meant hope.

The training was well planned. We reviewed subjects like daily maintenance, triggers, internal warning signs, and crisis plans for ourselves. Each action had its own action plan. We practiced in front of the group. At the end of the week, we had a wonderful celebration. Mom and Dad couldn't come as Dad was sick. Sister Lucy came, much to my surprise. Sam said he could not get off from work.

My dad's health was failing; he'd had a stroke, diabetes, and had lost one kidney to cancer. I spent a lot of time at the hospital, supporting my mother. Dad was in the hospital during Christmas. His vitals were failing, but on January 1 he insisted on having a stent put in his kidney. He talked the doctors into doing the procedure. Dad did not want to die. The cancer doctor told my mother and me that Dad would have to go to a nursing home after he was released from the hospital. My brother and mother arranged for him to go to Henrico Rehabilitation, near my parents' home.

He was in a corner room with windows. That morning after the stent was inserted, the doctor called a family meeting. Daddy was near death. He slept, we talked; every child, grandchild, and great-grandchild was there. Late that evening, my mother thought he was asleep and said to him, "Joe, do you know my name?" Out of that deep sleep, he awoke, pointed his finger at her and said, "You're Alyce Margaret Tedesco Budjinski and don't you forget it." He passed into God's arms very shortly after that. We all surrounded the bed, and said Our Father and Hail Mary. Dad passed on January 2, 2006.

Chesterfield County scheduled me to go on a trip to Portland,

Oregon, to mentor several people at a mental-health conference in the fall. At first I felt I was needed at home with my family; things just didn't feel right. Sam would go off on weekends, claiming that he was playing cards with friends. I'd call and find he was nowhere near where he'd told me. A couple of times he said he was going to see his mother, but when I spoke to her, she said he was not there. It was not like him to lie.

I was asked to be a spiritual director on an all-men's Cursillo team. It met every Sunday for two to three hours. Sam wouldn't miss me as he was always wrapped up in sports and beer. During the formation, I had the need to see a spiritual director myself, I asked Father Peter Creed from Saint Olaf's Church in Norge if he would meet with me for an hour a month; he agreed.

I prepared my talks meticulously as this was nothing like being on a woman's team. The men got down to business at hand, with limited pleasantries. I was the only woman on the team, so I gave them the feminine side of each subject. Each week one of the spiritual directors gave a reflection. There were five spiritual directors on the team—a priest, a deacon, two laymen, and me.

The weekend took place in February 2007. The reason I remember it so well is because when I arrived home late one Sunday night, Sam was on the telephone talking about a woman he'd been seeing. The next day I confronted him, but he denied it. When I unpacked groceries, I found the box for a lady's watch at the bottom of the bag. I was angry. I checked his cell phone records; he'd made many calls to a woman from work. I asked him to leave. He slept on the sofa until he found a place. He drank a case of beer a night, and I was living in hell.

I was determined to find a good divorce lawyer, stay in my house, and not go into the hospital because of this man. I called my therapist and saw her once a week. I decided to make myself a daily inventory, a sort of journal. Every night I wrote down what I would do the next day. The daily inventory had space where I could grade myself from 1 to 10 on anger, depression, anxiety, self-esteem, energy level, mood, socialization, eating, and, sleeping. I included time for exercise, humor, medication, spirituality, and daily hygiene. I added details like the music I was listening to and gave myself personal affirmations. I set aside a small space in my home to journal and pray. I used this tool faithfully every day.

The tool worked well in crisis situations, like when I went to the bank and there was no money in my checking account or savings account, and my equity line was maxed out. My black Labrador and I became good friends. One of my coping skills was to take her for obedience classes.

Sam and I didn't talk much, and when we did it became a yelling match on the phone. I couldn't hide the hurt I was experiencing. The year was a series of highs and lows, trusting God and being hurt by Sam. Many friends listened through my tears.

Going to Cursillo events every two weeks became part of my life, a part I looked forward to with joy. The men on the February team sent me McDonald's cards, prayer cards, gas cards; one of the men put a pass code on my computer to prevent Sam from taking all the money out electronically again.

Some of the time I spent with my mother, now a widow and living in the past. Some weekends I stayed with her.

Late in August, I called one of my friends from the printing company. He said he wasn't surprised how things had worked out with Sam. We spent time together, but I wouldn't call them were dates. We were just good friends spending time together.

I applied to do a presentation called In Our Own Voices (IOOV) for the National Alliance for the Mentally Ill (NAMI). This was a two-day workshop in North Richmond. Most of the attendees stayed in the hotel, but I was close enough to go home each night.

In IOOV we talk about our dark days, acceptance, treatment, coping skills, our successes, hopes, and dreams. I knew I could do this; I like to speak in public. I wondered if this was the right time to talk about the dark days of my illness rather than the dark days of divorce that affect my illness. Receiving a stipend was an incentive to start this venture.

I was excited to go to a graphics art banquet in Williamsburg with my friend. I dressed up in a long, black, velvet dress; had my hair and nails done; picked out jewelry, and I was ready to go.

Father Pete had a candidate for the next Cursillo men's weekend, and he wanted me to meet him and be his sponsor. I met him at the same hotel where the graphic arts banquet was held. Father Pete didn't tell either of us that we were both going through divorces. The man clearly was uncomfortable to be in a motel lobby. We talked about our faith, where we were on the journey. It appeared that we'd both thought about reconciliation with our spouses, but that wasn't working out for either of us. We went over his Cursillo application, and he said he would send it in.

I met my friend, and we walked into the large dining room. There must have been more than five hundred people; I knew a few from the printing company. The dinner and company were wonderful until the keynote speaker walked to the podium. All of a sudden I couldn't eat. What was I to do? I told my friend that I knew the speaker, and I was very uncomfortable.

I decided to approach him. This was the man I had stalked many years before. I asked if he knew me, and he looked like he'd seen a ghost. I told him I was manic in the days I'd stalked him. I apologized over and over. He accepted my apology. I felt a huge weight lift from me. I was so sorry for my behavior all those years ago. I was able to make amends. When I told my friend of this wonderful opportunity, we danced and partied. We closed down the bar talking, and I went home feeling free.

Grace sets us free.

Blowing bubbles at the NAMI walk.

Chapter 20
GRACE TO MOVE ON

In organizing my presentation, I needed a visual to explain the idea of the separate parts that made up my wholeness. I made a poster of a large pair of eyeglasses. On one side of the glasses, above the bifocal line, I wrote my name; below the line I wrote the symptoms I had gone through since the divorce started, and there were many. I was angry, depressed, grief-stricken, sad, confused, anxious, and blaming. On the bridge part of the glasses I wrote the names of the new tools I'd collected: IOOV, Cursillo method, Al-Anon, dog-obedience classes, and WRAP. The other side of the glasses had a list that indicated how I felt after applying the tools to my life: improved self-esteem, confidence, justice, and keeping my trust in God, no matter what. The eyeglasses had two stems—one for internal supports like my family, and prayer, the other for external supports like my friends, support groups, and work. Having it in black-and-white confirmed that I'd accomplished something lasting, which I could use to keep depression from taking over my life again.

I'd been talking with Jimmy, a man I met at the Cursillo. It was what I would call friendly banter. He had a strong New York accent and was from New York City. He was a cradle Catholic, who had been to Catholic school from elementary through college. He had been divorced twice and had three grown sons. He attended a Cursillo men's group reunion in the west end of Richmond. He had just moved to Richmond from North Carolina.

Jimmy facilitated a divorce care group at his church, and went to AA two or three times a week. He had been sober twenty-six years. He was working full-time, had a convertible sports car, and attended Mass each week, where he served as a lector—my kind a guy. I had seen him around the prayer groups, but at the time he was seeing someone in Northern Virginia. When the timing was right and his other relationship had ended, we had our first real date.

We were on our way to Williamsburg, and I asked if he had ever visited a cloistered convent. He hadn't, so I directed him to the Poor Clares in Barhamsville. That impressed him; then we went off to the Olive Garden and a tour of Yankee Candle. On the way home I asked him to take me to Lowe's, where I purchased a yellow-handled hatchet. On our first date, we went to a convent, a candle factory, and a hardware store. We had a few laughs, and laughter is good.

Two years of battling divorce lawyers persuaded us that going to court was the best way to settle matters between Sam and me. The first day was filled with grueling, painful, testimony, and it wasn't pretty. My lawyer was ready with evidence, including maxed-out credit cards; credit cards in my name that I'd never applied for; Sam using the equity loan on the house I'd owned before I married him to purchase a Harley Davidson for his girlfriend; and the list went on.

The judge held Sam and his lawyer in contempt of court for delays and lack of preparation. The two lawyers and the judge held a meeting without Sam and me, which was fine with me because I was shaking and praying. My priest came and sat in the back row for moral support and prayer.

The outcome was in my favor, but it wasn't over. Sam filed for bankruptcy, claiming he could not pay what he owed and wanted to use the remaining equity in *my* house to resolve *his* bankruptcy. When we had been married three years, he needed money for education and equipment to realize his dream of opening his own digital-printing business. I'd refinanced the house to fund this venture into digital printing, and that is how his name got on the title of the house.

I had to hire a bankruptcy lawyer to save my house. The day I met with the bankruptcy lawyer, I met with my priest first; we prayed for all parties involved in the bankruptcy. Then I went to the lawyer's office, and I was still. There was a little irony in that this was a digital conference; none of us were in the same room. My lawyer asked the bankruptcy court to dismiss the case. That was on a Monday, and on Thursday, the case was dismissed, and I still live in my log home.

Jimmy supported me through all of the stress associated with the divorce; for the first time, I was not alone. He had medical issues of his own, and I supported him through them as well.

I went to a Lenten mission at Saint Olaf's and the Redemptorist priest held a "letting go" ceremony. He asked us to put our loved one's hands in God's hands. I closed my eyes and put each of the babies I had lost into God's hands. I was set free!

Work was transitioning to digital medical records. I needed more support because that turned my work world upside down. I had to learn how to put all the records pertaining to a consumer into a new system, using a method so foreign to me, it might as well have been Greek! It was a slow process, but I was bound and determined that it would not beat me. I prayed over that computer every day.

I believe God places people in our lives for a reason. Chesterfield Mental Health hired someone who already knew the program and sat right next to me. He became my best buddy. My age was not in my favor; my younger peers picked up the new system as if it were second nature. I'm not there yet with digital media, but I'm better than when I started.

In telling my story I became free. Free to know who I was. Free to accept that the most important people to know in my road to recovery are me, myself, and I. Free to know that with hope in positive outcomes and through the Grace of God, all things are possible!

CHAPTER 22
GRACE TO ANSWER THE TOUGH QUESTIONS

ATTENDEES AT MY workshops ask questions about my recovery. I find this is a good way to share. The answers in this chapter are based on my perspective and experiences. The topics are those that have helped me connect the tapestry that is my journey of hope with my journey of grace.

Q: What activities can one would pursue to get well from a mental illness?

A: Keep learning new skills as life changes, and add activities that help you control as much as you can, such as:
- organizing your time
- establishing a daily routine
- using a daily inventory
- reading a positive affirmation each day

Q: How can you keep the mental illness from defining you?

A: Say to yourself, "I am more than this illness." List all the things you were able to do before your hospitalization, like drawing, singing, exercising, bicycling, or walking. Then go out and do some of them. You will be surprised at what you still can do. I did ceramics and won first place at the state fair for a chess set that I painted.

Q: I have heard that light helps depression; is that true?

A: Yes, this is true. Exposing the retina of the eye to light for twenty minutes a day has been known to lift depression, so get out into the light. Do not dwell in darkness; it is not good for the mind or the soul.

Q: Does volunteering help?

A: Serving others or giving back to the community has always helped me. Letting go of being self-absorbed has connected me to other people who have struggles as well. You are not alone. In helping others, we help ourselves.

Q: Does having a pet help with anxiety?

A: I believe when you accept responsibility for another living being, you are on the way to recovery.

Q: Does ECT (electric convolution treatment) really help major depression?

A: I know people who say that ECT treatments changed their lives forever in a positive way. Others did not have as positive of an outcome. That is a decision for you and your psychiatrist.

Q: Why do you think your Catholic faith had such a large impact on your recovery? (This question, asked at one of my workshops, startled me a bit.)

A: I never lost my faith in Jesus Christ. Reading scripture gave me the strength and courage to trust in the Trinity, the Father, Son, and Holy Spirit. The Catholic faith offered me confession, absolution and the Eucharist in its true sacred application.

Q: How do you stay positive without being a Pollyanna?

A: My journey was not always a positive experience. I tried to walk on both sides of the fence, but that didn't work. Positive energy attracts positive people, and those are the people I wanted in my life. Sometimes the positive feelings came through a movie, a singer, a lecture, books, or going to conferences. At times, it was from going to church and hearing just the right homily. Committing to a positive outlook can open you to negative reactions from others who will never understand. You have to prepare yourself not to listen to ridicule from negative people; remaining positive is your only answer.

Q: When resentment and bad things happened, how did you control your emotions?

A: That is why I pay a therapist. I have been going to the same therapist since 1985. We worked through those issues of resentment; the person they really hurt is you, as the other person doesn't know your pain.

Q: What does a therapist do for you?

A: Sometimes she is a sounding board, and I can figure out the issue by myself. At other times, she questions my behavior and the consequences of that behavior. She has followed my activities throughout the years and is aware of the patterns that have resulted. I have to remember she is not my best friend—I pay for her services—but she is friendly toward me, most of the time. Sometimes she presents me with a challenge or question to ponder or recommends reading material or a movie. We have been through divorces, weddings, education, and family members' deaths.

Q: What kind of reading material do you recommend?

A: My list is endless and includes a lot of self-help books, spiritual material, and fiction. I also enjoy reading about the Amish and the lives they lead, autobiographies, and biographies. I watch movies with spiritual, moral, ethical, and religious themes.

Q: How did your family and friends support you doing your recovery?

A: My parents were my biggest supporters. I have three brothers who have their own families. Most of the time, they came to see me in the hospital. I had to encourage them not to fear the stigmas. It got to the point if anyone asked my parents where I was, I told them to tell them I was in the hospital. If the family member didn't ask, there was no need to make a special phone call to say I was in the hospital. I was invited to all family functions and was asked to be a godmother during this time. My friends kept in touch and still do. One of my friends, who was not bipolar but very interested in mental health and spirituality, came to the support group on a regular basis. My prayer group met each week after I got off work at 10:00 p.m. or at lunchtime before I went to work. This band of three prayed and encouraged me to stay on focus, spiritually and health-wise.

Q: Did any words or phrases interfere with your journey of recovery?

A: Did they ever! Anxiety. Worry. Profanity. Obsession. Addictions.

And people with negative attitudes: Don't tell me I can't do this because I have a mental illness. I will find a way to make it happen!

Q: When you facilitate a WRAP class, what is in your toolbox?

A: I keep ten items in my toolbox.
1. A carpenter's level to remind me to stay level-headed
2. My therapist's card
3. A daily calendar
4. Bubbles, as I cannot talk and blow bubbles at the same time
5. A small Bible
6. Pens and pencils
7. Paper
8. Colored pencils
9. A furry and warm scarf (usually yellow), as I don't like to be cold
10. $5.00 so I never run out of money

Q: Which quote do you find comforting on your journey of grace?

A: "Diseases can be our spiritual flat tires—disruptions in our lives that seem to be disastrous at the time, but end by redirecting our lives in meaningful ways." Dr. Bernie Siegel

Q: What questions would you ask your therapist or psychiatrist?

A: I see a therapist every six weeks for forty-five minutes to an hour for cognitive therapy. I usually go with a list of events or issues that has bothered me since our last session. The appointment with the psychiatrist lasts about ten or fifteen minutes, if I'm lucky. He is all about medications. If I have an update on my medications, I give that to him. If I am taking an over-the-counter medication (OTC) I advise him about that. For example, my primary care doctor suggested an arthritis medication for my wrist and elbows. I also started taking a vitamin. I added both to my list of medications. I believe being honest with your therapist and doctors, especially if it is bad news. Let them know if you are going through a change of environment, new stresses, change in sleep habits, if any of your warning signs have come up since last visit, about your work or home life. Is your anxiety level up? Will a future event make you anxious?

Q: Money is always an issue with me, and I don't like talking about it to anyone. What do you suggest?

A: Create a budget in a notebook. Write down every outstanding bill. Keep the notebook current; pay the amount on the account; and write it down as paid and the date. Accept a feeling of accomplishment when you check it off. If you are talented enough on the computer, build a spreadsheet. Find a method that works for you.

Going through the divorces were tough. I accounted for every penny, nickel, and dime in the notebook. Peanut butter and jelly sandwiches made pretty good lunches. Find the thrift store and salvage stores in your neighborhood. G W Design and Sal's Place (Goodwill and the Salvation Army) have some really good deals. Check around; you will be surprised to find different prices for the same medication at different pharmacies. Write everything down in the notebook.

Q: What are some causes of stress?

A: Time pressures. Lack of mobility in one's life. Lack of a job or job security. Life changes. A need for approval. The death of a family member. Conflicts over values. Stress can be as complicated as a divorce and as simple as a cloudy day. What is key is not the stress, but what you allow to become a stress.

Q: What is a common sign of stress in one's life?

A: Increases in physical or medical issues; problems with relationships; negative thoughts and feelings; bad habits or addictions; exhaustion and fatigue.

Q: How can I combat stress?

A: Take inventory of your symptoms. Have a plan for when stress arises. Use positive affirmations. Exchange bad daily habits for healthy adventures. Exercise is cheap. Put one foot in front of the other, and take a walk. It's free and reduces depression.

Q: How do I start asking personal questions about my family history of mental and physical illness?

A: Make a family tree of the relatives of both your parents. Include parents, grandparents, siblings, aunt, uncles, and cousins. Circle the ones with heart issues in red, diabetic problems in green, kidney issues in orange, cancer in pink, and mental issues in blue. Put a double blue circle around drug users and alcoholics. The more you know about your family's illnesses, the more likely you'll be to prevent it in your own life. Start to GEL (Genetic, Environment, and Learned).

Q. Do you keep in touch with your stepchildren (love children)?

A. Yes, all of them call me, or e-mail me or Facebook me. During the holidays, we keep in touch. I have two granddaughters and one grandson and, at last count, five great-grandchildren.

Daily Personal Inventory

DATE_____Mon. Tues. Wed. Thurs. Fri. Sat. Sun.

Appointments: _____

Things to do: _____

Circle - 1 being the worst/ 10 being the best

Anxious - 1 2 3 4 5 6 7 8 9 10	Low Self Esteem 1 2 3 4 5 6 7 8 9 10
Distracted 1 2 3 4 5 6 7 8 9 10	Energy Level 1 2 3 4 5 6 7 8 9 10
Happy 1 2 3 4 5 6 7 8 9 10	Socialization 1 2 3 4 5 6 7 8 9 10
Sad 1 2 3 4 5 6 7 8 9 10	Eating 1 2 3 4 5 6 7 8 9 10
Angry 1 2 3 4 5 6 7 8 9 10	Sleeping (hours) 1 2 3 4 5 6 7 8 9 10

Journal/Artwork/ Positive Affirmations

Exercise:

How long and where

_____

Humor:

What and were?

_____

Medication

AM-Noon –Evening-PM

_____

Prayer/Meditation

_____

Prepared by
Maryalyce Poole
1/1/10

CPSIA information can be obtained at www.ICGtesting.com
Printed in the USA
BVOW02s1301280414

351918BV00001B/8/P